GARDENING
the SOUTHWEST:

How to care for your land while growing food, beauty and medicine

by Carole Tashel

copyright ©1999 Carole Tashel, Healing Earth Publications

ISBN 0-945401-24-8

I dedicate this book to my parents,
in gratitude for their
generosity and support.

FOREWORD

Most of the material in this book originally appeared in "The Natural Garden" column in *Crosswinds*, which I wrote for three years. The inspiration came from the land—the greater New Mexico landscape and the small piece of it entrusted to my care. My background includes over ten years of teaching classes in herbal medicine, and eight years of gardening (landscape and vegetable).

A big thank you to Steve Lawrence, editor and publisher of *Crosswinds Weekly*, for getting me started and keeping me going on this project. I am indebted to many people who generously shared their knowledge with me as I researched the topics in this book. Blessings upon Rick Phelps, Mark Wood, Bill Isaacs (how we all miss your wisdom!), Bob Pennington, Tracy Neal, Gail Haggard, Linda Wiener (especially for her entertaining bug stories), Gordon Tooley, Michael Melendrez, Brett Bakker, Patrick Torres, John Jeavons, all my herb and Permaculture teachers, and a host of other friendly people too numerous to list. Thanks also to Linda Braun and Gershon Siegel for encouragement and design assistance, and to my cheering section—dear friends and family.

I hope you, my readers, enjoy this book. And may your encounters with life in your garden be ever harmonious.

Carole Tashel
Santa Fe, Winter, 1999

TABLE OF CONTENTS

PART 1:

Vegetable & Landscape Gardening

HOW TO BECOME YOUR OWN LANDSCAPE DESIGNER:
Six Ways to Make Your Garden Look Better

Creating a garden isn't something you do in a week. It's a complex design adventure which takes place over time. Though you may not think you're an artist, in your garden you get to act like one, balancing form, line, color, texture and so on.

Attention to the following principles will help beautify existing gardens and should give beginners somewhere to start.

1. Discover What You Like and Why You Like It.

A beautiful garden is a powerful place which can evoke an emotional response. Do you already have an image of how you want your garden to look and feel? Would it be soothing in its elegant simplicity? Or a stimulating riot of color? Do you dream of a wild, mysterious place you could get lost in? Would subtle fragrances of honeysuckle, wisteria and mock orange make you swoon?

If you aren't really sure what you want, try some judicious snooping in established neighborhoods, or join tours of local gardens. Contact botanical gardens, rose societies, gardening clubs and xeriscape councils to find out where the action is. Then shamelessly borrow others' ideas as you plan your landscape.

When you see something you like, find words to explain what you like about it. This will help you choose the right plants later. Perhaps the contrast of deep purple (meadow sage) and pale yellow (moonshine yarrow) knocks you out. What is the mood of the garden, and how is it achieved? Do you feel expansive walking among sculptural trees, whose leaves give dappled shade to a fragrant ground cover? Notice how the juxtaposition of different shapes and textures can create a dramatic effect. And don't forget that your primary design lessons are always available along country roads, in forests and wild-flower meadows.

2. Create Year-Round Interest.

As autumn's stunning colors fade, leaves lose their grip, revealing the skeletons of shrubs and trees. By December each year, Northern New Mexico's freezing temperatures bring soft-stemmed plants to their knees, and the garden disappears. What then?

If a quarter to a third of the shrubs and trees are evergreen, your garden won't be invisible. A piñon with some character is worthy of winter attention. And some deciduous trees are anything but boring without leaves. Take for example the gnarled bones of an old apricot tree dusted with snow.

Ornamental grasses maintain their fountain-like forms in the winter, and some assume a handsome reddish color. See what you think of maidenhair grass or fountaingrass.

Aside from plants, winter interest is created with lichen-covered rock walls, sculptures, a bench or a boulder.

3. Encourage Complex Webs of Garden Life.

Some landscaping books advise limiting the number of plant species to 15. I'm sure I've got well over 100. (Some rules ought to be broken.)

When the diversity found in nature is imitated in the garden, the result is increased plant vigor and resilience, and much more color and texture. What's more, you can choose plants based on their purpose, not just their appearance. For instance, herbs like thyme draw beneficial insects which eat bugs you don't want. Arroyo lupine and purple prairie clover feed the soil and surrounding plants as they grow. Wild hyssop (*Agastache cana*) provides late summer color, while its bright pink flowers drive hummingbirds to distraction.

4. Soften Hard Edges; Shun Straight Lines.

This principle and the next reveal my preference for an informal, natural-looking garden. Lay out garden beds in irregular shapes, with sinuous, flowing lines. Experiment with new shapes by laying heavy rope or a hose on the ground; squint your eyes and imagine.

Trailing stems can be allowed to drape over walls and creep between rocks. Wooly thyme and Turkish speedwell will soften and surround a flagstone path. One easy way to achieve a relaxed look is by using plants which "naturalize." This appropriate expression means the plants spread in an unpredictable way, without help from you. Some great choices include showy Navajo tea, California poppy, blue flax, bachelor buttons and black-eyed Susan.

Inhibit the reflex to control everything, and let plants roam, mingle and rub shoulders with each other. The outcome may delight you.

5. Plant in Natural Groupings.

Nature doesn't plant in perfect symmetry—why should you? Instead of filling a bed with evenly-spaced plants, stagger clusters of three, five or seven plants each. I read of a woman who threw out a large handful of bulbs in the fall, and planted them where they landed. You get the idea.

Take an inventory of the heights of your established plants. Does your garden include ground-level, mid-story (shrubs) and upper-story (trees) plants? Adding the missing level easily turns a ho-hum garden into a really pleasing environment.

Spend some time on your roof, where it's easy to see the flow of your lines, how the groupings work, and any imbalances in the density of plantings.

6. Introduce Elements Which Unify Your Garden.

Repeating plant material is one way to accomplish this. For example, I planted 15 (perennial) blackfoot daisies as a ground cover throughout two beds separated by a flagstone path. These drought-tolerant, foot-high white daisies bloom all summer and visually tie the beds together.

An extremely effective way of creating a cohesive landscape is with meandering paths. If the path has a destination, such as a small pond or a bench in the shade, so much the better. The garden becomes a place to move through and live in, rather than something to look at passively. Winding paths can also define areas and beds, give access for maintenance, and provide a sense of mystery.

Some gardens are unified through color. Ask your nursery for a list of blooming sequences so you can have color throughout the growing season.

GOOD LUCK, AND ENJOY YOUR MISTAKES

Be willing to make lots of mistakes. Then try to correct them. I didn't discover what worked until I was looking at what didn't work. Many mistakes can be remedied by moving plants to better locations, some by adding plants, and some only by finding another home for what you thought you liked. (It's tricky to move trees, especially evergreens, so get some advice on this one.) ·

I admit I didn't know any of this stuff five years ago. But with patience and determination, through trial and plenty of error, my garden simply happened—slowly. Perhaps if I had read an article like this at first, it might have taken less time. Then again, what's the hurry?

HOW TO HAVE A
THRIVING DESERT GARDEN
Or...Don't Throw in The Trowel

To some people, gardening in the Southwest sometimes seems like an exercise in masochism broken only by occasional gloating over fleeting successes. Our enchanting weather features intense sunlight; low humidity and meager rainfall interspersed with monsoons or hail; temperature swings with spring frosts as late as May 20; desiccating, relentless winds; and winter freezes. Whew.

All this leads directly to poor alkaline soils (and to gardeners pulling their hair out). But by choosing appropriate plants and helping them get well established, you can save your hair and have a satisfying, self-sustaining landscape. Don't think "appropriate plants" means two yuccas and a cactus in a sea of gravel. The harmonious textures and forms that people find so endearing in the Southwest—soft native grasses, silvery shrubs, feathery foliage and colorful wildflower accents—can nourish you in your garden. Here are a few tips.

First, everything's easier if you choose plants known to prosper here—those crusty characters who prefer their soils on the alkaline side, don't mind being nipped by a late spring frost, and aren't too fussy about how much water they get to drink. And if you aim for a "xeriscape" (from Greek *xeros*, dry), an attractive landscape with a majority of plants that aren't very thirsty, your reward is to chop at least half off your water bill. Speaking of water bills, you can't miss with a hardy, drought tolerant lawn of buffalo or blue grama grass. Kentucky bluegrass needs at least 30" of water per year to stay green; we get maybe 12 to 14".

You won't be happy without some shelter from sun and wind, and neither will your plants, so think about this one early on. The house itself can be clothed and cooled with trellises or ramadas covered with sweet-scented honeysuckle or juicy grapes. Both vigorous, fast growers, they're forgiving of placement near hot walls. While waiting the three years or so for them to give the cover you seek, plant scarlet runner beans, an annual which can grow 15' in a season. As a bonus, you can eat the flowers or the beans (but not both).

Plant lots of trees and shrubs—they form the underlying framework of the landscape and give shelter to smaller plants. Try the locust tree (*Robinia* varieties need the least water), fast growing and well adapted to our climate. The airy foliage gives light shade, appreciated by even those plants designated for full sun...and hail won't rip it to shreds. Prefer denser shade? Many varieties of green ash can deliver it to you.

There are so many wonderful easy-to-grow shrubs—a couple of my fragrant favorites are big sage (*Artemisia tridentata*) and English lavender. A note for patient people: smaller specimens adapt more easily than very large ones, surpassing them in size in one to three years. You'll save money, too. (Starting in a one gallon pot, my big sage grew 4' tall and 6' wide in four years. I'm gloating.)

So you've got the right plants—now what? Sorry, but even the toughest plants need a little coddling for the first two growing seasons, minimum. That means a decent childhood in reasonable soil, with proper watering and fertilizing. No matter which problem soil you have—decomposed granite, sandy soil or the adobe brick variety (clay)—the solution is the same: add plenty of organic stuff like alfalfa meal, humus or compost, and/or fertilize with GroPower. Skip the peat moss—you can achieve workable soil here without denuding peat bogs somewhere else. Rather than improving soil in a small area around each plant, do it in an entire bed, to equalize the movement of moisture and encourage roots to venture out further.

It's hard to believe, but there's almost five times as much evaporation as precipitation here, so it makes sense to get water exactly where you want it with drip irrigation systems or soaker hoses. Use other sprinklers only on windless days, early in the morning. Water established plants slowly, thoroughly, and *infrequently* (looser sandy soils more often—they don't hold water well). You'll encourage deep root systems which give plants the edge over the vagaries of our weather. (Smaller new plantings may need more frequent drinks.) Shading or mulching the ground cuts way down on evaporation; the ultimate, permanently charming mulch needing almost no care is a tapestry of ground covers like creeping thymes, Turkish speedwell, sedums, etc.

So there really are ways of bringing the desert to life. As you persevere in coaxing plants to thrive in this dry land, may your successes be more than fleeting.

RESOURCES

Expert advice on do-it-yourself drip irrigation systems: In Santa Fe, **The Firebird,** 1808 Espinacitas, 983-5264. In Albuquerque, **Sisco,** 4610 McLeod NE, 881-4050.

The Enchanted Xeriscape, free booklet on water-wise plants, (800)-WATER-NM.

How-To Guide to Xeriscaping, a free, 48-page booklet published by the Water Conservation Office in Albuquerque, 768-3655.

Larger nurseries stock the excellent books by Judith Phillips, to inspire you in planning your Southwestern garden.

Plants of the Southwest catalogue: great photos and thought-provoking observations. Santa Fe, 438-8888; Albuquerque, 344-8830.

Best of all, see mature plants in a garden setting: **Santa Fe Greenhouses** demonstration gardens, 2924 Rufina Street, 473-2700. In Albuquerque, check out **Xeriscape Park**, 4600 Osuna NE, or the landscaping at **Lovelace Clinic**, 5400 Gibson Boulevard SE.

◉ ◉ ◉

UNMAKING THE DESERT, YARD BY YARD

The concept of "healing the earth" may sound like an overwhelming and clearly unmanageable task for the average individual. But truly effective change can begin on a small scale, with you and me, outside the back door. In the drylands, there are ample opportunities to practice the art of earth healing. For example, take the issues of dwindling groundwater and alkaline, water-repellent soils. As is often the case in the natural world, these two problems are closely related.

Soil's ability to receive and absorb water depends partly on the spaces within it. (Healthy topsoil is at *least* 35% air!) Mulch extends an open invitation to earthworms to go to work, creating tiny channels. When rainwater enters these spaces, organic activity starts, creating a receptive, sponge-like structure. Water then *stays* in the soil longer. The formula for healing is completed with plants, their roots burrowing sometimes many feet underground, their leaves falling, adding to the rich humus stew. Voilà...nature begins to come to life.

Sheet Mulching

Fall is the perfect time to mulch the entire garden and prepare new areas for spring planting. All kinds of ready-made mulches are available, but "sheet mulching" surpasses them all. (Imagine sitting by the fire, pitchfork and spade in the garage, while your soil improves itself under the snow.) This method yields moist, fertile loam appropriate for vegetable gardens or flower beds. No need to dig up those weeds or grasses—just compost 'em.

This no-digging approach is easy: You build a sort of mulch-sandwich and just lay it on top of the dirt and weeds that you want to transform. Construct the mulch a layer at a time, soaking each layer as you go. First soak the ground. Then overlap the edges of a layer of heavy brown cardboard (white contains dioxin), removing tape or staples. Cardboard's the easiest to work with, but non-colored newspaper will do. Next add about four inches *fresh* horse, chicken or sheep manure, and top off with six to 12 inches of loosened straw. The entire sandwich will settle appreciably within a month, and be just a little above grade by spring. (The straw eventually breaks down and is hidden by plant foliage.) If winter moisture is sparse, soak thoroughly once a month. Worms, active when protected in cold weather, are crazy about the glue in the cardboard. The manure's nitrogen helps break down carbon in both cardboard and straw. All winter, tuck kitchen scraps under the cardboard to delight your worms. By spring, it's ready to plant—just push straw aside and place seeds or larger plants. Beware of being shocked, though, by the sight of rich, black soil, full of life.

Cover Crops

A cover crop may be the ticket when reclaiming bare, eroding or heavily-weeded land. Sometimes called green manure, these crops are grown for three to six months. (They're great to grow in empty vegetable beds over the winter, too.) When they're tilled under early in spring, they decay and enrich the soil with humus (and nitrogen, if they belong to the pea family, e.g. vetch or clover). Wait two or three weeks, then seed the area with native grass or food crops. Check with nurseries or folks familiar with Permaculture methods about the best approach for your specific needs.

Swales

Rainwater, even New Mexico's measly amounts, is an incredible resource. Though badly needed to enliven soils and plant life, in drylands water is often viewed as a destructive force or an unwelcome waste product. Bare soils, thinned by winds and battered by heavy rains, don't allow water to penetrate, so our saving grace rushes out of reach into the arroyo or storm drain. (About 80% of rainfall on open land is lost this way.) But with some planning, literally thousands of gallons can be persuaded to seep into the thirsty earth.

"Swales" are shallow ditches of any length (usually in a series) which intercept water and allow it to infiltrate slowly. (To help you understand their placement, picture yourself on sloping land, looking downhill. The swale goes *across* the slope—like the path of a skier traversing but not going downhill at all. Try a small one to see how it works.) Use the dirt from the ditch to make a small berm on the lower edge. Shrubs and trees planted on swale edges prevent evaporation by keeping water down in the root zone. Better yet, including such plants as Western sand cherry, native plum or New

Mexico Privet gives birds and other wildlife something to eat in the winter. If you own at least an acre of land, the State of New Mexico is eager to help you heal it, and offers inexpensive seedlings (*see* Resources).

Harvesting Rain

The perfect opportunity to capture and store rainwater awaits you on your roof...for every 1000 square feet of surface, almost 7500 gallons of water can be collected each year here (based on 12" rain per year). Directed by downspouts into a variety of tanks, barrels or even large cisterns, the precious stuff can then be brought to the garden via gravity flow or a small pump. (When the first rainwater flowed through my hose end, my excitement ran pretty high.) Two cautions: Screen any open tanks to prevent wild critters from taking a fatal swim. Very small tanks can split when water stands in them in freezing weather, so it pays to consider a system with large storage capacity. (400 gallon stock tanks are great for this.) (*see* page 87)

Whether you live on three acres or have a city yard the size of a postage stamp, you can experiment with these possibilities. Then, on a small, manageable scale, you and I can revitalize the soil and begin to return thousands—no, millions—of gallons to our water table, while slowing depletion of the dwindling aquifers. Whether only 10 people do this, or 1000, for earth's sake, let the healing begin!

RESOURCES

Introduction to Permaculture, by Bill Mollison, Tagari Publications, Australia, 1991. Full of useful ideas on everything from garden layouts to sheet mulching and swales.

Permaculture is a complete design system (including ethics and philosophy) for creating sustainable human environments. (*see* page 52) For information on classes, call **Permaculture Drylands Institute**, 983-0663. In Albuquerque, call the **Permaculture Guild Hotline**, 281-4871; in Taos, call Brigid Meier, 758-1318; in Los Alamos, call Bonnie Gordon, 672-3115. To find help in using Permaculture techniques in your garden, call the **Permaculture Institute**, 455-0270.

New Mexico Forestry & Resources Conservation Division, P.O. Box 1948, Santa Fe, NM 87504-1948, 476-3325. Offers inexpensive shrub and tree seedlings to be used for erosion control, conservation, windbreaks and wildlife plantings. Call in early fall to receive a brochure, and order early—they often sell out.

Permaculture Drylands Journal, No. 23, August 1995, "Enriching soil through cover cropping;" send $6.00 to PDJ, P.O. Box 156, Santa Fe, NM, 87504-0156.

HOW TO CREATE A GREAT GARDEN ON A TINY BUDGET

If spending big bucks on a garden is not an option for you, you can still have a wonderful garden. It requires a little more involvement and patience on your part, but it's not hard. Here are some tips.

The Planning Phase

Whether you're redoing an existing garden or starting from scratch, you'll need to make some design decisions. First familiarize yourself with the plants and design possibilities. Once you have some of your own ideas, an hour spent with a landscape designer will be more productive and worth your money. Albuquerque residents can contact the Albuquerque Garden Center's Master Gardener Hotline, 292-7144, for free help. Though Master Gardeners aren't all designers, they can advise on plant choices.

Preparing the Ground

For areas which will be gardened intensively and need rich soil, you can let nature make your soil (instead of buying topsoil) by "sheet composting." (see page 11-12) Moistened layers of weeds, kitchen and yard wastes, newspaper or cardboard, manure and straw are allowed to sit on the ground for six to eight months and turn miraculously into the best soil you've ever seen.

Compost is an essential ingredient of the garden. The cheapest option (resulting in the best product) is to make your own. (see page 23-26) Free compost materials are everywhere—in bags on the street on trash pickup day, in barber shops (hair), markets (spoiled produce), restaurants (coffee grounds) and stables.

If you don't make your own, you can save from $13 to $40 or more by buying compost "by the yard" (27 cubic feet), rather than by the bag. Delivery usually costs much more than the compost, so borrow a truck. Most places will gladly load your truck. Some suppliers sell Back to Earth or mushroom compost in bulk; others make their own from scratch. The quality of commercially-made compost varies greatly, so if you're new to gardening, ask what it's made from, get samples and seek an experienced gardener's opinion.

Some bulk compost suppliers: **Santa Fe**: Payne's Organic Soil Yard, 424-0336; Santa Fe Greenhouses, 473-2700. **Albuquerque**: Soilutions, 877-0220; Barela Landscaping Materials, 877-8522. **Taos**: Blossom Garden Center, 758-1330. These places sell a large variety of items in addition to compost.

Composted manure is useful as a soil amendment and conditioner.

(Avoid steer manure—it's too salty.) Places to get free horse manure include stables, riding schools, horse boarders, fairgrounds, etc. If you're unaware of sources near you, look in the Yellow Pages under Feed Dealers, and they should be able to help.

Let manure age before using it in the garden. Wet the pile thoroughly, cover it with a tarp, and let it cook for six months. Some people report that nasty weed seeds like bindweed or goatshead are introduced by manure. Ask questions before buying.

Straw (*not* alfalfa or hay) is an inexpensive, cooling mulch, much cheaper than using only compost. It can be mixed with nitrogen-rich materials for composting, and whole bales can protect tender seedlings from wind, or form the walls of raised vegetable garden beds and compost piles. (Actually, hay is a nutritious mulch, but many object to the alfalfa seedlings which may come up. Also, rabbits will eat it, which may or may not be a problem for you.)

Since most locally available straw comes from southern Colorado, it's hard to find it free in our area. Check with feed stores to see if you can rake it up from the floor of their storage barns. Ask if they have any broken or moldy bales to give away. Though most straw bale home builders have plans for their broken bales and "waste" straw, it doesn't hurt to ask.

The Hardscape: Paths, Rocks, Trellises, etc.

Instead of buying expensive redwood trellises, experiment with large, dead juniper branches. You'll get to look at something interesting in the winter when the plant dies back. Another trellis alternative is 4x4 or 6x6 inch square wire mesh. Use a spacer where it's attached to the wall so the mesh stands about two inches out from the wall, giving vines plenty of room to twine in and out. Concrete reinforcing mesh is widely available at places like Furrow's, but it rusts. If you object to that, look for galvanized or steel wire instead. Call fencing stores and ask if you can purchase wire by the foot (rather than in a 150-foot roll).

If you need gravel or rock, look under "sand and gravel" in the yellow pages. When constructing gravel paths, rather than lining the path with weed barrier cloth, choose the no-cost option—layers of overlapped cardboard or very thick newspaper.

I think the most attractive path material is shredded bark. I'm not talking about those uniformly-sized, dark brown pieces of bark. I mean the stuff tree trimming services grind up. It's soft and natural-looking and doesn't get icy in the winter like flagstone paths. (To prevent or delay weeds and grasses from showing up in your path, line as in the gravel paths, above.) Call tree services to see what they have available (often large amounts for very little money).

Some lumber yards and landfills offer shredded bark free or at low cost.

Again, get samples from all the sources, then make your decision. To avoid problems, don't mix bark into garden soil or use as a sole source of mulch.

If you plan to construct terraces, a sandbox for the kids, or raised beds to grow vegetables, locate free pallets and take them apart. I found one made of oak. In some cases, low cost, rot-resistant materials are dangerous. Don't use railroad ties—they contain toxic creosote. "Treated lumber," "pressure-treated lumber" and "landscape timber" translates to "poisoned wood." Though the sellers won't tell you (or claim it isn't true), this wood allows arsenic, chromium and copper to leach into the soil and is unhealthy for children to sit on.

Saving Money on Plants

With a restricted budget, you'll want every plant you buy to thrive. Choose tough, mostly native plants. Try to let go of the desire for instant gratification: buy small plants. A two- or three-foot tree can catch up with a six-footer in two or three seasons; plants in two and a half-inch pots, if cared for properly, can grow fast. And timing is important. For best results, wait until September to plant. The weather is more forgiving, and nurseries always have fall sales. Ask nursery employees to show you the root systems on smaller plants (especially two and a half- and four-inch pots) to make sure they're fully developed.

Find out where the plants were grown. Most nurseries specializing in native plants—like Agua Fria Nursery (Santa Fe), Plants of the Southwest (Albuquerque and Santa Fe) and Santa Ana Garden Center (Bernalillo)— gather local seed and grow their own stock. Some larger nurseries do this as well. Such plants may adapt more easily than those shipped in from other states.

Here's a list (by no means complete) of the plants I'm most impressed with. They all give a lot, some by ease of care, others by growing fast, or multiplying their numbers and so on.

Ground covers: Turkish speedwell, creeping thymes, most sedums, catmint. **Wildflowers**: blackfoot daisy, paper flower, most Penstemons, showy Navajo tea, chocolate flower, Jupiter's beard (red Valerian), sulfur flower, globe mallow, Maximilian's sunflower. **Vines**: silver lace vine (prune back heavily once a year so it won't eat the house and children), grapes, Hall's honeysuckle (needs some water). **Shrubs**: Rosa rugosa, mountain mahogany, chamisa, all the Artemisias, three-leaf sumac, lavender. **Trees**: locusts, oak. Grasses: blue grama, *Stipa tenuifolia*, Indian rice grass.

Interested in giveaways? At the end of the season, some nurseries like Stark Brothers, (800) 325-4180 or Bear Creek Nursery, P.O. Box 411, Northport, WA 99157, (509) 732-6219 may have bare root trees they need to get rid of. And seed companies often give away out of date seeds for landscape and vegetable plants. Most seeds last much longer than just one year. In late summer and fall there are seeds to collect from your own and friends' wildflowers.

Do you own at least one acre? Are you interested in mass plantings for preventing erosion, constructing windbreaks, or to feed wildlife? The New Mexico State Forestry offers seedlings at very low cost, but you must purchase a large quantity at once. Call 476-3325 to find the office nearest you. Bear Creek Nursery also offers smaller quantities at good prices.

There are ways to make many plants out of one. Some perennials and most bulbs can be dug up and divided every few years. Cuttings can be taken from stems, leaves and roots, and grown into new plants. For elementary explanations on these techniques as well as layering, budding and grafting, see the Sunset *Western Garden Book*.

Network and Save

You can cut costs by joining with others. Neighborhood associations and community gardens often get nursery donations or discounts for group projects. Garden clubs present opportunities to exchange plants, seeds, materials and money-saving ideas.

Talk to landscaping class instructors, and check out the Permaculture Breakfasts in Albuquerque (281-4871) or Santa Fe (983-0663). People who teach permaculture and landscaping classes often need demonstration sites—you may get free advice, plants, installation of a French drain or other free labor by volunteering your site for the class. Or throw a sheet-composting or path-laying party for your friends.

You needn't be a dumpster diver to score the stuff you need; just look in Santa Fe's *Thrifty Nickel* or Albuquerque's *Quick Quarter*. Another great resource is the Trash to Treasures column in the Sunday *New Mexican's* "Neighbor" section. This recycling bulletin board lists what you need or what you have to give away. People are exchanging manure, plants, wood chips, pallets, bricks and more.

If creating a low-budget landscape sounds like it might keep you too busy, there is another way. My friend Linda thinks the answer is plastic flowers: they're inexpensive, and need only an occasional dusting.

◈ ◈ ◈

From Dust to Loam:
GREAT SOIL & HOW TO GET IT

If you long for a beautiful garden, filled with happy, undemanding plants, the place to start is Ma Earth. Due to New Mexico's sparse rainfall, soils here are prone to damage, deficiency and alkalinity; but with a little human intervention, the earth repairs herself, pronto. And when plants get what they need from the earth, they are less attractive to insects. Simple techniques like mulching and adding compost can transform dusty dirt into fertile ground, with no need for concentrated fertilizers. Sure, a vegetable garden requires richer soil than a landscape of drought-resistant native plants— but the basics are the same.

The needs of soil don't differ much from human needs: food (compost and humus), shelter (mulch), and water. Meet these requirements, and dirt comes to life. Literally. (Since healthy soil harbors living beings, pesticides are verboten.)

So what IS great soil? And how do you get there from that lump of clay in the back yard?

The operative word here is ROT. Beneath the soil, decaying organic matter (humus) enriches and supports microscopic exchanges among bacteria, fungi, minerals, organic acids and water, helping nutrients dissolve and become available to plants. As earthworms and other tiny critters excrete sticky, gummy substances, soil particles bind together into cohesive structures. Together with the web of tunnels formed by worms (a minor miracle themselves), this allows the soil to absorb and hold water (up to four times as much as without worms) without becoming soggy.

To have the moisture necessary for rot, you need mulch—a two- to four-inch organic covering (like straw, grass clippings or mature compost) that keeps soil cool and moist and denies weeds a foothold. Or, plant ground covers like thyme, sedum or pussytoes—they accomplish the same thing. This is all you need to do to set the stage for long-dormant worm eggs to come to life. I know it seems impossible, but trust me. I've seen the miracle myself. One caution: Keeping mulch out of contact with the base of trees and shrubs prevents rodent, insect and fungal infestations.

Good Compost

Good compost that contains humus is the backbone of any garden soil— it prevents clay soil from turning into an adobe brick when wet and/or compacted, and it helps sandy soil or decomposed granite hold more water. Make your own or use "Back to Earth" or "Nature Life" organic cotton burr compost. Mix some in, and top off with at least one inch *each* year (up to three inches in a first-year garden). Don't skimp. It's great stuff. It pays to be heavy-handed when applying these organic materials, because the hotter the climate, the faster soil organisms consume the goodies you give them.

Even if you don't have a compost pile, there are two very simple ways to feed your hungry soil: Combine kitchen scraps (no meat or fats) with a little water in a blender, pour on the soil, mix in; cover with mulch. Or dig (unblended) scraps into an area where soil will remain undisturbed for about a month. Keep it mulched and moist, and worms will show up to transform wastes into rich soil. (If your mulch is thick enough, worms will stay active throughout the fall and winter, when they lay eggs.) It makes more sense to put food where it's needed than to burden a septic system by throwing it into the "garbage" disposal.

If you dig down to plant a tree or shrub and find a whitish layer, powdery or hard as a rock, you've struck caliche (basically a mass of calcium). Yes, you must drill through it or break it up. Then add *really* generous amounts of compost, humus and, after planting, mulch.

Soils here are already too alkaline, so avoid chemical or highly concentrated fertilizers, as their phosphates and nitrates add still more mineral salts. (However, a fertilizer like GroPower is 50% humus, contains soil bacteria, and causes no problems.) Worse, nitrogen eventually seeps into the groundwater, posing a real danger of contamination. It's much easier to pollute an aquifer than to clear it of poisons.

Now you know the most important secret of a successful garden: rotten soil!

RESOURCES
Let it Rot!, The Home Gardener's Guide to Composting, by Stu Campbell, Storey Communications, 1990, $8.95.

What Every Gardener Should Know About Earthworms, by Dr. Henry Hopp, Storey Publishing, 1978, $1.95.

How to Grow Soil:
THE BIOINTENSIVE METHOD
OF GARDENING

We've blown it, as far as the seventh generation goes. Our soil is in terrible shape. Based on present agricultural practices, we may have, at best, only 50 to 100 more years of world soil productivity. And that's not just in other countries. The U.S. loses over three billion tons of topsoil each year.

It's no secret that massive, mechanized farms, propped up with chemicals and government subsidies, wreak environmental havoc and suffer from steadily decreasing yields. Despite the pleasant illusion of plenty in overflowing supermarket aisles, it's my belief that in 10 or 15 years, the compost will begin to hit the fan. What then?

A Way to Create More than You Consume

Enter John Jeavons and the Biointensive Mini-Farming method. Part of the solution, Jeavons believes, is returning the bulk of food production to small, local farms and backyard gardens. The smaller the scale, the better the earth can be cared for; once established, soil fertility can last indefinitely.

Jeavons' precise, easy method is rooted in techniques practiced by cultures such as the Mayans and ancient Chinese. He also has drawn on the more recent European horticultural traditions of Biodynamic and French Intensive gardening. The result is a way to

> "The nation that destroys its soil destroys itself."
>
> FRANKLIN D. ROOSEVELT

build rich topsoil which improves year after year. More food is grown in the smallest possible space, while decreasing all costs and conserving resources.

Long-term goals of sustainability—creating a genuinely self-perpetuating garden—are woven throughout Jeavons' teachings. His ideal is to reduce (or eliminate) outside inputs (such as the purchase of seeds or soil amendments) and meet all the needs of the garden, as well as the gardener, on site. (This may include income crops as well, such as cut flowers.)

The Biointensive method asks us to shift the way we think about gardening. "Don't grow plants, grow soil," Jeavons repeatedly reminds his students. Good soil is about half air, yet surprisingly full of life. It has what's referred to in gardeners' jargon as "structure." It's glued and sewn together as a result of the activity of billions of macro- and microorganisms as they go about their life processes, forming tunnels, excreting sticky or threadlike substances, etc. This kind of soil is like a living, breathing sponge and can hold a tremendous amount of water in reserve. That means water use can drop as much as 75 percent—certainly a boon for dry lands like ours.

One Key is Double Digging

"Adequate air," says Jeavons, "is one of the missing ingredients in most soil preparation processes." A technique called double digging, explained fully in Jeavons' book, thoroughly aerates the soil to two spades deep (24 inches), without mixing topsoil with subsoil. After the initial digging, the soil structure that develops is disturbed as little as possible. Beds, around three to five feet wide and of any length, are created, rather than the usual rows.

Did you groan thinking about digging your soil 24 inches deep? The initial investment in time and energy is more than repaid as roots proliferate and effortlessly stretch out to get more of what they need. Plants are more drought resistant, drawing on the soil's deep water reserves. Also, heavily mulching for six months before digging helps a lot. (There are some suggestions in the book on double digging rock-hard soil.)

Compost: The Longer it Takes, the Better it Gets

Amazingly, plants get about 96% of what they need from air and water. The gardener's responsibility is to add the other 4%, which consists of nutrients contained in organic matter and organic fertilizers.

At Jeavons' research farm in Willits, California, he's concluded that carbon (after it's composted) is the key to sustained soil fertility. This fact is never mentioned at garden lectures or in the magazines, eclipsed by the focus on NPK (nitrogen, phosphorus and potassium). Carbon is present in dried-out stalks, twigs, woody stems, straw, etc.

I can't overestimate the importance of knowing how plants get nourished in an optimal situation. Residues of composted carbon in the form of rich, black humus provide a durable, year-round food supply for soil microbes, which predigest nutrients for the plants. (Microbes are also the pharmacists of the soil, making antibiotics which plants draw upon to stay healthy.) As minerals and nutrients are gradually broken down, they are dissolved in water, and the plant roots actually drink their meals.

No wonder conventional agriculture is not working. Pesticides kill the life in the soil, the earth is continually disturbed (no structure *there*), and fertilizers "feed the plants" with hollow chemicals and rapidly break down organic matter in the soil. What hubris, to ignore nature's ways so completely!

Some Like it Hot, Some Cold

In a manner characteristic of this culture's love affair with speed, gardening magazines boast, "Now you can have rich, dark compost in just 14 days." Well, the Biointensive method of "cold composting" takes from three to twelve months. Temperatures stay much cooler than in "quick" piles which are turned frequently. Jeavons claims hot piles can burn off carbon too fast (thereby wasting this critical element) and kill off a lot of microorganisms.

The cold compost pile is built with a higher than usual ratio of dry (carbonaceous) materials to moist, green (nitrogenous) materials, and soil is included as one of the layers. Soil helps cool the pile and contributes "starter" microbes. The end product is sustained-release, superior humus, which holds water to at least 75% of its volume.

A great tip for those in no hurry whatsoever: A pile composed almost exclusively of carbon-rich twigs, branches and dried-out stalks takes up to TWO YEARS to break down, but makes primo long-acting compost. Start one now, as a garden investment.

The Crops

Biointensive gardeners plant from 60 to 70% of their space in compost crops (corn, sunflower, amaranth, quinoa, wheat, etc.) which generate high-carbon stalks and straw. Happily, these crops also provide ample calories and/or protein.

You see, when we import straw and manure from other farms to make compost, we deplete those lands to enrich ours. The goal is for each growing area to produce enough compost to maintain the fertility of that soil. (Jeavons' research organization is still working out the fine points on this one—stay tuned.)

Commonly grown vegetables (tomatoes, lettuce, carrots, broccoli, etc.) provide little carbon for composting and few calories for the gardener. Jeavons quips, "You need to learn to grow ALL your food, not just your yuppie chow!" In other words, not just gourmet salad greens, but carbon, calories and protein as well.

There are two more important elements of the Biointensive method: companion planting and diagonally offset, close spacing of plants in the beds. Please check out Jeavons' book for more details. If you're intrigued by this method, it's best to try all the techniques in one small area (three by three feet) while continuing your usual garden practices.

I feel sustainability is worth striving for on an individual level, no matter how convincing the illusion of plenty appears. There are rich rewards to be reaped, with an impact far beyond the personal.

RESOURCES

Ecology Action, 5798 Ridgewood Road, Willits, CA 95490, (707) 459-0150. Non-profit research and educational organization founded by John Jeavons. Call for information about workshops and study opportunities. "Bountiful Garden" catalogue available, featuring open-pollinated seeds, books and a series of informative publications.

How to Grow More Vegetables (than you ever thought possible on less land than you can imagine), by John Jeavons, 10 Speed Press, Berkeley, 1995. This is the fifth edition of the 1974 classic, revised and expanded, $19.95 postpaid worldwide from Ecology Action.

THE LAZY GARDENER'S GUIDE TO COMPOSTING

One of the best times to make compost is after the first fall frost, when gardeners are inundated with piles of leaves, frost-killed vegetation, and other garden waste. Instead of sending this stuff to the landfill, why not transform it into an unequaled soil amendment by composting it?

People make compost in bins, barrels, pits, piles, trenches and everything in between. Some methods are considerably more precise and labor intensive than others—and involve hoisting pitchforks full of half-made compost from bin to bin, with a finished product in as little as two weeks. But if you're in no hurry, compost happens without doing much of anything. Here's what you need to know to get a good product with the least amount of work.

Compost Demystified

Compost is simply decayed organic matter. The transformation of garbage into black gold is accomplished by hordes of tiny organisms, which may include bacteria, fungi, actinomycetes, mites, springtails, pillbugs, and of course, worms. They do their work in the presence of organic materials and moisture. Pretty simple, right?

Indeed, some folks just toss whatever they have in a heap, and eventually it breaks down. The trouble with this approach is that it can be messy and often smells. Which brings me to an important element for a more socially acceptable compost pile—air. Here's a look at each ingredient necessary to make compost.

1. **Air**: Organic matter will decay under either aerobic (with air) or anaer-

obic (without air) conditions. Aerobic composting is far more aesthetically pleasing, and if done properly, produces no offensive odors. Anaerobic decay, on the other hand, generates compounds which give rise to morbidly fascinating aromas, like hydrogen sulfide (smells like rotten eggs), cadaverine and putrescine (don't ask).

2. **Organic Materials**: If it once lived, or is a byproduct of something that lived, it can go in a compost pile (with some important exceptions). Organic materials are of two types—carbon and nitrogen. Microbes use carbon for their fuel, but they can't digest it unless they have adequate nitrogen to munch on. Carbon-based matter includes bulky (usually dry) vegetation like flower stalks, corn husks, straw, dry leaves and so on. Their coarse texture allows air to flow through the pile. Wood chips and sawdust are the most concentrated sources of carbon, and must be balanced with adequate nitrogen in order to break down. Shredded (moistened) paper and cardboard (which can't be recycled) may be composted, as long as they aren't coated and colored.

Nitrogen-based matter includes fresh leaves and lawn clippings, garden trimmings, fresh manure, coffee grounds, kitchen scraps, etc. (Dried alfalfa, kelp, blood, bone and fish meal are also nitrogen sources.)

Any combination of carbon plus nitrogen is okay. I once made a pile from only straw and manure. More variety in materials, though, leads to a greater diversity of organisms in the finished product.

What to leave out: Wood ashes (too alkaline), plants which inhibit the decomposition process (walnut, cypress, juniper, pine, acacia), Bermuda grass, bindweed (wild morning glory), disease-infected plants, cat and dog manure, meat, salt, oils and dairy products. Commercial cow manure is too salty (cattle are often fed salt for weight gain). Weeds actually add important nutrients, but mature seeds may persist in the finished compost. Place any such weeds in a black plastic bag in the sun for a few days to kill the seeds.

3. **Moisture**: The pile should be about as moist as a wrung-out sponge. Too much moisture suffocates aerobic microorganisms and results in a stinky pile. Too little moisture slows or stops the decaying process.

Build a Straw Bale/Redworm Compost Pile

Between the cave man waste heap and a carefully tended Perfect Pile are various intermediate approaches. My current favorite is a straw bale-enclosed pile in which redworms help break down materials. With a little care in the layering process and a cover (a tarp works well) to prevent drying or waterlogging, I don't have to turn the pile or monitor moisture levels. Here's how to do it.

Choose a level spot at least three feet by three feet. With a pitchfork, slightly loosen the soil underneath. Place straw bales on their sides to form the walls. First lay coarse brush, small branches, whole sunflower or corn stalks on the bottom in a three-inch layer, to help aeration. Then make one- to three-inch alternating layers of carbon-rich and nitrogen-rich matter. The smaller the pieces, the faster they break down. Layers of carbon can be somewhat thicker than nitrogen. Every few layers, sprinkle one quarter-inch of garden soil—or better yet, some homemade compost. This jump starts the pile with microbes. Lightly moisten each layer as you go.

After making a few layers, include a big handful of redworms (also known as manure worms or red wigglers). Redworms are a different breed than fishing worms or earthworms, and they eat their weight in a day. They increase their numbers quickly, rove the pile, and they're hungry.

The straw bales insulate against winter cold and keep the pile from drying out in the summer. Place a thick layer of straw on top, and don't forget the tarp. Unlike other exposed piles, worms stay active year round. A compost pile can be built all at once (if you have a lot of materials) or gradually. I add kitchen scraps every few days and keep other layering materials (straw, horse manure, etc.) nearby, covered in the winter so they won't freeze.

As the pile "cures," it shrinks. After about six months, move aside one of the straw bale walls and see if your compost is ready.

What's So Special About Compost?

Though organic matter composes up to only five percent or less of the total volume of the soil, it's essential to garden health and productivity (especially for vegetables). Why? First, nutrients are released from compost slowly, as plants need them. An excessive concentration or sudden burst (as with chemical fertilizers) of available nitrogen makes plants more susceptible to disease and insect damage. So using compost is like giving plants three square meals a day, rather than a huge binge every few months.

Second, compost is decidedly alive. As soon as it's applied, the microbes and worms get busy improving soil structure, adding air spaces and increasing water-holding capacity. Even better, microbes make antibiotics which plants draw on. Recent studies show that when compost is used on the surface as mulch, many common plant diseases are prevented.

It's not hard to make compost. But when you see that rich, dark, crumbly stuff and sniff that sweet, earthy smell, you *will* find it hard not to brag about your own.

RESOURCES

Backyard Composting Made Easy, free brochure by New Mexico

Environment Department, Solid Waste Bureau. Call Greg Baker at 827-2780.

Organic Gardening Magazine's "Compost Corner" column. Each issue offers three or four instructive and entertaining submissions by enthusiastic composters sharing their ideas and methods.

Redworms: In Santa Fe: **Suchi Solomon**, 984-2109, eves. until 10, or **Willie Lambert**, 982-3169. In Albuquerque: **Jim & Karen Brooks**, 281-8425. Other locations: Call the **Cooperative Extension Service**.

❖ ❖ ❖

THE STRAIGHT POOP ON FERTILIZERS:
Feeding Your Southwest Landscape

Plants, like people, need the right amount of quality food for consistent growth and resistance to disease. Accordingly, each year gardeners flock to nurseries and stare at a bewildering variety of powders, pellets and potions which promise perfect plant health. Which of these products do you really need?

To answer that question, let's first remind ourselves of how the expert, Mother Nature, feeds plants.

Death Gives Life to the Soil

The circle of life is based literally on the slow decay of "organic matter," a euphemism for dead plants, animals and insects. As these morsels are digested by worms and billions of microorganisms, a dark colored substance —humus—is formed. Plants love humus and thrive in the presence of it. Another result of the breakdown of once-living matter is the liberation of nitrogen and mild organic acids. A little acid in the soil is a good thing—it dissolves minerals so plants can slowly assimilate them.

Simple enough, but here in the Southwest we have special problems with this process. For one, everything that's not nailed down blows away, so decay is a moot point. For another, even if there were something lying around, it wouldn't rot with such scanty rainfall. And since our rot quotient is so low, soils remain alkaline rather than acid. The minerals needed by the plants are present but unavailable, tightly held in undissolved complexes.

To give decay (and the resulting humus it forms) a chance to happen, you must add the organic stuff yourself and then cover it with mulch so every bit of moisture that falls sticks around as long as possible. You'll also be adding some readily assimilable minerals.

So slow decay of diverse, naturally-occurring elements is the ideal. In our created landscapes, however, we often fall short of that goal, so we end up buying simplified products to substitute for the highly complex natural compounds which are more than adequate to nourish plants. Here's a brief guide to those products.

A Basic Primer: Nitrogen Phosphorus & Potassium

First a caution: The best method for feeding vegetables (or pampering plants not adapted to this area) differs from what follows—check with nurseries for specifics.

The series of numbers you see on fertilizer bags (e.g., 2-11-0) refers to percentages of nitrogen, phosphorus and potassium. These three major nutrients, abbreviated "NPK," are essential to plant health.

Nitrogen (N) (along with phosphorus) is the most likely to be deficient in our soils. It's the major building block of protein and results in leaf growth. Nitrogen is generated by decay of organic matter, which is made of protein. But it can also be carried by rain from the air into the ground, provided by bacteria living on the roots of certain plants (e.g. clover, lupine, scarlet runner beans), and extracted from the air between soil particles. Some sources: Composted manure, alfalfa meal and compost 1-2%, cottonseed meal 6%, fish meal 10%, blood meal 12%.

Phosphorus (P) gives plants energy for strong root development and for the growth of flowers, fruits and seeds. Some sources: Colloidal ("soft rock") phosphate 2%, bone meal 11%. Don't let the numbers mislead you. The percentages of phosphates refer to the amount available in the first year. Bone meal is used up in six months, whereas colloidal phosphate is still releasing nutrients four or five years later. There are other forms of phosphate, but colloidal phosphate is best for alkaline soils.

Potassium (K) promotes a steady flow of nourishment throughout the plant. Essential for strong stems and roots, it helps plants adapt to stresses such as drought, insect damage and temperature extremes. Some sources: Seaweed 1%, greensand (an ancient marine deposit) 5%, most (composted) animal manures and compost 1-2%. (Ashes are high in potassium—potash—but are overly alkaline. Don't use them).

Aside from the major nutrients, plants require smaller amounts of the minor nutrients—calcium, magnesium, sulfur, iron, zinc and manganese, and a host of trace elements. Some sources: Rock dust, kelp meal, alfalfa meal, greensand, seaweed and, of course, well-made compost.

Organic fertilizers (made of natural substances like fish, manure, bone, rock, kelp, etc.) generally have low "NPK" numbers, and deliver nutrients slowly, as occurs in nature. Avoid highly concentrated, entirely synthetic products. Some contain as much as 33% nitrogen, 44% potassium, etc. Sure, they make plants grow bigger and greener, faster ... but there's a price. Too much of one nutrient imbalances the others. Even worse, a big dose of unbuffered chemicals overwhelms the life of the soil and stops humus formation.

What about the fancy stuff? The technology of gardening offers exotic fertilizers (bat guano, Squid-Doo), granules to help soil retain water, products to wake up slumbering soil bacteria, break up, catalyze, enliven and stimulate your soil. These products *may* make a difference, but could distract you from the basics, which still work fine: Feed thy soil; mulch thy soil.

Standard Nursery Feeding Recommendations

So now at least you can look intelligently at all those bags of stuff at the nursery. But how do you feed a garden? Nurseries usually recommend feeding landscaped areas twice a year, adding, at the minimum, N,P,K, granular iron and compost. Nurseries can advise you how much to use. Fertilizing in early to mid-May gives plants a boost just as they're beginning to leaf out. Feed again early in the fall, but DO NOT apply any fertilizer with more than 7-8% nitrogen, or you'll stimulate growth and prevent plants from entering into dormancy.

If you're not ready to create your own NPK combination, use the all-purpose fertilizer Gro-Power Plus (5-3-1). It boasts trace elements and a humus base that conditions and nourishes the soil. Occasionally add seaweed or alfalfa meal for more trace minerals.

Good compost is the backbone of the garden. Depending on how it's made, it contains small amounts of all major and minor nutrients and is rich in trace elements. (Continue to supplement with NPK and iron, though, unless you make perfect compost.) If you don't yet make your own, Back to Earth or Nature Life are brands recommended by many nurseries. Or try Soil Foods—a certified organic cow manure-based compost inoculated with beneficial microbes. Call (888) 393-7845. Mushroom compost is a luxury item, best reserved for fussy plants.

Peat moss has been used widely to improve retention of water in the soil; it's really unnecessary to rob peat bogs when compost and earthworms can do the same thing. Besides, peat moss lacks nutrients.

Imitating nature does pay off in the long run. If you start supporting the life in your soil, your plants will become surprisingly resilient, and eventually you'll need less fertilizers.

❊ ❊ ❊

THE ART OF
TRANSPLANTING

While plants are usually relieved to get out of cramped nursery pots and into garden soil, they detest being uprooted and moved to another spot. Transplanting is a gamble—some plants don't survive it—but there are ways to help plants adjust to their worst nightmare.

Roots Are Where It's At

You will encounter two basic types of root systems: an anchoring tap root, or a network of thin, fibrous surface roots. Most plants adopt one form or the other, although you will find plants which have both types. The larger the plant, the more extensive the root system, and the more risky it is to transplant. But even some small native perennials like *Liatris* and desert four o'clock, have large, deep taproots, and moving them is seldom successful.

Further, most plants develop cooperative relationships with other nearby plants as well as with organisms in the surrounding soil. With all the important stuff that happens in the root zone, it's no wonder that disturbing this area—inevitable during transplanting—can threaten the equilibrium and life of a plant.

When to Transplant

Good timing is a prerequisite to success. Ideally, the plant should be in a dormant or semidormant phase—in other words, transplant between October and mid-March. An early spring bloomer should be moved in the fall; late spring or summer bloomers can be replanted in early spring.

Work during the coolest part of the day, preferably early evening. Plant juices flow downward at the end of the day, allowing energies to be replenished. Plants can use this energy to re-establish roots in their new environment.

For even more refinement in timing, transplant during the waning moon. Plants naturally form more rootlets at this time. Sure, few people have the luxury of fine-tuning to this degree, but at least now you know.

What to Transplant

Easiest to move are small to medium-sized plants which have been in the ground only a year or two. Even small trees can be transplanted successfully. But don't even think about moving fully-established native shrubs or mature trees, especially evergreens. Most conifers are never fully dormant, have immense root systems, and may take years to recover.

If you are forced to move a large tree or shrub, it's sometimes suggested to "root prune" several months before relocating it. This involves marking a circle around the plant that's ten times the diameter of the trunk at ground level, and cutting straight down to a spade's depth. In response, the plant grows a new set of surface "feeder" roots within the root ball. However, don't get your hopes up: the tree or shrub still may not survive being moved.

How to Transplant

Prepare the new hole *before* unearthing the candidate for it. The roots of transplants grow outward for some time before they grow downward, so loosen the top foot of soil in an area from two to three times as wide as the plant to be moved. Then mix in some soil from healthy, established garden areas. This inoculates the new location with worms and other soil organisms.

Your goal in digging up the plant to be moved is to get as many and disturb as few roots as possible. Watering the plant the day (or a few hours) before you move it makes it easier to dig, and prevents the root ball from falling apart. For small perennials and shrubs, dig straight down, as deep as the plant is wide, just outside the outer perimeter of foliage (called "the drip line"), then underneath, as deep as the plant is wide. For trees, figure nine inches width of root ball for every inch of trunk diameter. To carry a very large root ball, roll it onto a piece of burlap.

If there's any delay getting your charge into new ground, cover the root ball with a damp rag and place in the shade. A dried out root is a dead root. In sandy, fast-draining soil, transplanting may be less successful. Roots must venture two or three times further than in clay soil, in search of water and nutrients. Besides, a sandy root ball tends to crumble and fall apart.

To plant, the bottom of the root ball should rest on solid soil, the top of the root ball even with the soil surface. Backfill the hole, add compost and mulch. Don't fertilize for at least a few months. You don't want the reduced root system to have to support extra leaf growth.

Stress Relief for Unsettled Plants

I read *The Secret Life of Plants* and realize how fully aware these green beings are. Transplanting is pretty upsetting to them, so I let my plants know my intentions and my wishes for their happiness. (I'm not so evolved that I ask their permission—they might say no.)

Immediately after moving the plant, water thoroughly. When all water has been absorbed, drench again with a dilute solution of Superthrive (10 to 15 drops per gallon water), which is available at any nursery. These vitamins and hormones help prevent transplant shock. (Superthrive is not a fertilizer.)

One drench is enough, unless the plant seems unusually stressed the next day. Diluted seaweed could be used the same way, and either preparation can be sprayed on leaves with good results. Be careful not to overwater, but make sure the plant doesn't dry out for at least a week.

Though it's less than ideal, sometimes a plant must be moved in warm weather. Always shade it and protect from strong winds until it recovers. Cover small plants lightly with straw, use sticks to build a shade teepee, or invent your own shelter. Just make sure the plant can breathe and doesn't overheat. My neighbor, who can successfully transplant almost anything, cuts holes in brown paper bags, then skewers them to the ground with small stakes. It looks funny but works well.

If you want to give the plant one less thing to deal with, place it with the same orientation to the sun as it had in the old location. Though most plants can and do readapt to different orientations, it's kinder not to ask them to do it.

It's amazing that transplanting works at all, given that a large specimen may end up with 10% (at best) of its root system. Up until a couple of years ago, conventional garden practice dictated pruning back the stems, even up to one third, so the roots wouldn't have to support so much above-ground growth. However, the latest advice is not to cut off any growth, since root-stimulating hormones are produced in the stem tips. Even in the summer, a transplanted tree, in its ultimate wisdom, will self-prune, dropping leaves it can't support, until it recovers.

If you've never tried transplanting, start with the easy stuff—small perennials, volunteer seedlings, vigorous young vines. Then have at it. It's a skill worth developing.

❖ ❖ ❖

HOW TO GET YOUR GARDEN READY FOR WINTER

In the fall, gardeners' thoughts turn away from growing and are focused on putting the garden to bed. All across northern New Mexico, extreme winter weather brings danger to unprotected plants. Here's what to do to insure that your garden comes through the coming winter in good shape.

Why Water in Winter?

The greatest risk to plants is extended periods of dry, cold winter weather. Though plants have shed their leaves and aren't actively growing, they still need water—especially trees and shrubs. And so do recent additions to the garden which haven't had time to develop generous root systems.

Snow satisfies some of the garden's thirst, especially when it remains on the ground, melting slowly. Consider though, that 12 inches of snow is equal to only one inch of rain. Unless it snows a foot a month, you need to get out the hose.

So twice a month in the fall, and once a month during winter, early on a sunny, relatively warm day, water slowly, thoroughly, deeply.

Along with watering, mulching is imperative to protect the winter garden. The best mulch is two or three inches of compost or fully-composted manure. It loosens soil, evens out alkalinity and adds organic matter while protecting soil from the elements.

The Freeze/Thaw Cycle

In February, when we're fed up with winter, we usually get a reprieve of warm weather, and go into denial, confident that spring's on its way. Then in March, the temperature plummets. It's hard on humans and excruciating for plants.

As water freezes, it swells, lifting the crust of frozen earth above the unfrozen ground below. As the ground thaws, the soil settles, but the plants don't, and roots may be partially exposed. Each succeeding freeze/thaw cycle heaves plants further out of the ground, breaking roots. This can happen even to established trees and shrubs. To prevent or reduce the severity of this damaging cycle, apply a thick mulch, which prevents frost from penetrating deeply.

Extreme temperature swings (and winter "sun scald") can also damage the trunk of certain deciduous, smooth-barked young trees (fruit trees, birch, etc.), until aging toughens the trunk. Some advise shielding the trunk with tree wrap.

Because trees breathe through their trunks, even in the winter, it's important to use a product which doesn't hinder air circulation. DeWitt Tree Wrap is the best product—breathable and white, which reflects the sun. Use wrap only in the winter, and be sure to remove it in spring as soon as the tree begins to leaf out. One non-wrap option for protecting trees is simple: stake some shade cloth on the south and west sides of the tree.

Build Soil While You Feed Plants

What do plants need in the fall and winter? Certainly not a lot of nitrogen, which stimulates leafy growth. Fall feeding is more about helping plants withstand winter stresses, encouraging root growth, and providing what plants will need just as they break dormancy in the spring. For instance, phosphorus is needed for flower, fruit and seed development, but it takes a while to break down. Adding it in the spring would be too late.

I prefer organic-based rather than chemical soil amendments because they're released slowly, are easier on plants and build soil tilth. Check out alfalfa or kelp meal, Gro-Power iron (with humic acids), greensand and colloidal phosphate. Any or all of these are fine to add in the fall.

What about lawns? Lawn fertilizers specially formulated for fall application (sometimes referred to as "winterizers") provide fair amounts of nitrogen for early greening, along with other plant-strengthening elements. However, for native grasses, which won't turn green until warm weather, winterizers are unnecessary.

Last Chance to Plant

If you just can't face the fact that gardening season is over, go plant something. But hurry, so the roots can grow a little before the ground freezes. Choose only containerized, hardy shrubs and trees with good root balls.

Many people are unaware that fall is preferable to spring for planting trees, shrubs and perennials. Plants can comfortably adjust in cool, moist weather, and they have six months to get ready for summer. As long as the soil isn't soggy, I plant until early November.

Santa Fe Greenhouses suggests planting pansy seedlings (not seeds) in late fall, mulching with one inch of mushroom compost, then waiting for the early spring show. And you can plant spring bulbs until mid-December.

Speaking of bulbs, it's easy to grow your own garlic. On October 15,  plant individual garlic cloves two inches deep and six inches apart in a sunny location. Harvest the bulbs the following July, after the tops begin to die back.

November is prime time to plant perennial wildflower seeds—they need winter's freeze/thaw cycles in order to sprout in the spring. For best results, stick to locally collected seeds, and choose species appropriate to your altitude.

More Fall Projects

• Reflect on this season's gardening successes and failures; indulge in wild fantasies for next year.

• Order seed catalogues for next spring's vegetable garden.

• Plan ahead for December's living Christmas tree: dig the hole now, and cover the dirt you dig out with a tarp so it won't freeze. Keep the evergreen indoors a maximum of 10 days, harden off in a protected spot outdoors, and plant on a sunny day.

• Do work that might kill you if you did it in June—build rock walls, dig water catchments, etc.

• Country-dwellers need to protect young seedlings and trees against marauding rodents who are ravenous when grasses are dormant. Wrap quarter-inch hardware cloth around trunks, or use one-inch chicken wire cages, depending upon the size of your local varmints. (I have jackrabbits as big as a medium-sized dog, willing to eat anything.)

• Set up feeders and put out fresh water to attract birds. In return, the birds clean your trees and soil of the destructive insects, grubs and larvae which were settling in for the winter. Birds also need high-energy suet in cold weather, and many appreciate apple and orange slices and a bowl of peanut butter. In rural areas, set up bluebird houses before mid-December, while you can still get the pole into the ground. Bluebirds start flirting as early as February.

❂ ❂ ❂

MEETINGS WITH REMARKABLE SEEDS:
Resources for the Vegetable Gardener

You might think that on a freezing January night, vegetable gardeners would be sipping hot cider in front of the fire. Wrong. They're feverishly fingering their next year's seed catalogues, planning their spring gardening extravaganzas. Though it's easier to buy vegetable seedlings from local nurseries, the extra effort required to grow from seed yields rewards for you and the planet.

On the practical side, after the initial investment in seed, you save money. Seeds stored in a cool, dry place last from one to three years, and six months of vegetables can be grown from about two dollars' worth of seed. Once you start generating and collecting your own seed, those vegetables are free.

Moderation in All Things Except Variety

Most U.S. diets are truly impoverished in terms of variety. Why, then, should gardeners limit themselves to the same old broccoli and zukes when they could feast on deep pink Thai tomatoes, scorzonera (oyster flavored roots) and mâche (corn salad)? But growing unique plants does much more than grace your table with beautiful shapes, colors and flavors. Variety has other implications.

Consider the Irish Potato Famine (750,000 perished), a hard lesson in plant genetics. The Irish were growing a single type of potato. When a blight was introduced from America, and the weather was uncooperative, the crops failed. This never would have happened in South America, where thousands of different genetic strains of potatoes are grown, each with different strengths.

Presently, the genetic base of U.S. crops is the narrowest in history, and losing ground steadily: By 1995, 85% of all varieties used in agriculture were extinct. This means less adaptability to changing conditions (and today's weather patterns are anything but stable).

This dismal picture is caused in part by agribusiness' love affair with monoculture (huge acreage of a single crop). The steadily shrinking number of small farmers growing traditional crops doesn't help either. But a much greater influence is the introduction of hybrid plants by large seed companies. Hybrids (a cross between two plant varieties) will not reproduce new plants identical to the parent. This obliges the customer to purchase another package of seeds. The net effect? Evolution of new plant varieties grinds to a halt. (There are, however, some excellent, vigorous hybrid varieties—no need to completely banish them from your garden.)

Many small seed companies nervous about the shrinking gene pool provide "open-pollinated" plants which do reproduce "true to form" (meaning you can grow next year's crop with this year's seed), and "heirloom" varieties, long prized for their flavor, vigor and adaptability. Thus, gardeners and seed savers create "backyard biodiversity" which is like survival insurance both in the garden and worldwide.

Dazzling Choices For Desert Gardeners

If the profusion of possibilities is too daunting, just choose a couple of plants that seem appealing. Order in January or February to avoid disappointment. Note: "Early" varieties ripen in the fewest number of days and are best suited to our short growing season.

Native Seeds/SEARCH, 2509 N. Campbell Ave., #325, Tucson, AZ 85719, (520) 327-9123 (Albuquerque, 268-9233). A unique resource for growers in low to high elevation deserts. This non-profit conservation organization has assembled a collection of seeds from traditional native growers in the Southwest and Mexico. Your purchase keeps these precious native seed stocks alive. To support the return of Pueblo farming, free starter seeds are available to Native Americans. Spring catalogues contain full seed descriptions.

Plants of the Southwest, Agua Fria, Rt. 677, Box 11A, Santa Fe, NM 87505, 438-8888 (Albuquerque, 344-8830). Open-pollinated, heirloom and modern varieties, all of which thrive in our region. A whopping 27 varieties of chiles (grow your own salsa) and a selection of traditional warm season vegetables, beans, corn, tomatoes, amaranth, quinoa, and selected heirloom vegetables.

Seeds of Change, P.O. Box 15700, Santa Fe, NM 87506-5700, (888) 762-7333. Organic seeds from New Mexico and Oregon research farms. Specific growing tips, many heirlooms, drought-tolerant and open-pollinated seeds.

Seeds West Garden Seeds, 317 14th St. NW, Albuquerque, NM 87104, (505) 843-9713. Specializes in fine heirloom vegetable and flower seeds for Western gardens, with an eye towards drought tolerance and ability to handle difficult soils and climates.

Ronniger's Seed Potatoes, Star Route 1, Moyie Springs, ID 83845. A delightfully simple specialty catalogue, featuring the largest selection of organic spuds in North America. (Whole "seed potatoes" are cut in several pieces before planting.) Delicious descriptions of each variety, and plenty of advice on all phases of growing, storing and cooking.

Bountiful Gardens, 18001 Shafer Ranch Rd., Willits, CA 95490-9626, (707) 459-6410. Over 300 open-pollinated seed varieties. This catalogue is an education in itself. Precise planting instructions (garnered from decades of testing in research gardens) increase your chances for success.

The Cook's Garden, P.O. Box 535, Londonderry, VT 05148, (800) 457-9703 Trial gardens and a test kitchen guarantee the dependability of these seeds. (Cool northern climates and high southwest deserts have enough in common so these plants work well here.) Be prepared for a staggering number of greens for Mesclun (a salad mix of young leaves such as chicory, sorrel, rocket and mâche). Unique items include a vegetable garden seed mix for kids, and two collections—"Windowsill Greens" and "Container Garden"—for those short on space.

Seed Savers Exchange, c/o Kent Whealy, RR 3, Box 239, Decorah, IA 52101. A non-profit, genetic preservation organization dedicated to conserving and promoting heirloom vegetables, fruits, flowers and herbs. Each year, SSE's 8,000 members offer the seeds of 12,000 rare varieties through membership publications. Revenue from seed sales is used for foreign plant collecting expeditions to areas such as Uzbekistan, Eastern Europe, etc., where traditional agriculture is practiced, and to maintain seed collections at their Heritage Farm.

Johnny's Selected Seeds, 1 Foss Hill Road, RR 1 Box 2580, Albion, ME 04910-9731, (207) 437-4301. A wide selection of organic seeds of high quality, many produced on their own certified organic farm.

GROWING FRUIT AGAINST ALL ODDS

Everyone loves fruit. Eating fruit you've grown yourself is especially thrilling. But growing it can be a relatively tricky, labor-intensive, long-range project—kind of like raising a child. What's more, fruit trees ask for three to five years of patience while they mature to bearing age. By using good judgment in placement, giving plants the right companions, and choosing varieties which are hardy in your particular climate, all that effort can pay off.

Juggling the Variables

Many factors influence the success of your plantings. It often pays to listen to the valuable tips of locals who have eaten fruit from their trees, and then imitate their placement, care, etc.

No advice could apply to every fruit grower in the diverse lands of northern New Mexico. However, climatic challenges fall roughly into two categories: too cold and too hot. Many areas (notably Santa Fe) suffer late spring frosts which ruin the blossoms. In this case, varieties which are "late bloomers" or have an extended blossoming period have a better chance of maturing their fruit. In areas like Albuquerque where springs are usually better behaved but summers are sizzling, more attention must be paid to placement and regular irrigation. Avoiding extreme conditions is advisable no matter where you live.

Consider, for instance, the "frost pocket." On any piece of land, the coolest air "drains" to the lowest point. That spot should be avoided in areas with late frosts; but it may be the best spot to cool down a tree in Albuquerque.

Trees Like Company

Most fruit trees need a partner (a different variety of the same species which blooms at the same time) in order to be cross-pollinated and become fertile. Curiously, even trees which "self-pollinate" bear more fruit with a partner.

Plants also like to hang out with other plants different from themselves. Why? They're engaging in the sharing of resources so characteristic of natural systems. More diversity translates into a healthier garden ecosystem, resulting in more fruit.

Here's how it works: One type of plant association is based on a trio; one plant that needs food, another that gives food, and a third that aids in pest control. Other additions might be plants that shade, cool or condition the soil, encourage earthworms, etc. For instance, near your fruit tree, you plant an Apache plume for the nitrogen it gives to the soil, cilantro for its early blossoms which attract ladybugs (which then go after aphids), and comfrey to shade and condition the soil. Add some bulbs (onion, garlic, daffodils), and you're on your way to a happy, extended family.

Predictable Fruit

In the interest of narrowing the dizzying array of choices, here's a sampling of what's worked exceptionally well for the fruit growers I interviewed.

Plum: The plum is extremely hardy, undemanding about soil, and the tree most likely to bear fruit, regardless of the weather. European plums (such as Stanley or Green Gage) bloom late, thus avoiding nasty spring weather. (A frost-free, protected spot is necessary for Japanese plums.)

Cherry: The sour ("pie") cherry is the winner in colder areas. It fruits in June or July, while you're still hungrily eyeing your other fruit. Sour cherry is one of the few tree fruits that self-pollinates quite well, and doesn't need a partner, thank you. Try the Montmorency—it produces large fruit which sweetens the longer it's left on the branches. (Birds love cherries. If netting or a scarecrow isn't part of your landscaping plan, plant a mulberry tree next to the cherry—birds like them better than cherries.) Sweet cherries may make it in Albuquerque.

Raspberry: This favorite offers nearly instant gratification (fruit within one year). With minimal care, it presents fistfuls of berries. Says Barbara Damrosch in *The Garden Primer*, "If I could grow only one fruit, it would be raspberries." I agree. My Heritage raspberries are thriving next to a low wall which gives shelter from harsh west sun and southwest winds.

Grape: Another easy, abundant producer. Put grapes in the hottest spot you have, then stand back. Each plant can yield up to 15 pounds of fruit. Choose Himrod (eat fresh, or dry for raisins) or Canadice—both varieties are seedless. Catawba is best for juice, since it has seeds and a tough skin; ripe fruits have an intoxicating fragrance on the vine. Thompson seedless may succeed in Albuquerque.

Apple: So many apples, so little time. Many varieties do well, but Golden delicious is considered most reliable. A vigorous self-pollinator, it escapes damaging frosts by blooming over an extended period of time. Experiment, if you like, with any of the over 1000 apple cultivars, but throw in at least one Golden delicious.

Peach, Pear, Apricot: I wish it weren't so, but these well-loved fruits can be tricky. Pear is most reliable—try the Asian or Bartlett varieties. Apricot and peach bloom early, and you know what that means. If you're up for the challenge anyway, try the Reliance, Red Haven or Belle of Georgia peach, and the Manchurian ("sweet pit") apricot. No guarantees.

Saskatoon: Known more plainly as the shadberry or service berry, the fruit resembles a blueberry, and was a traditional native food. A hardy type for northern New Mexico is *Amelanchier utahensis*.

So when it comes to growing fruit, an attitude of good-natured experimentation seems to work the best. And if you can't have your fruit, maybe you can settle for shade.

RESOURCES

Fruits & Berries for the Home Garden, Lewis Hill, Garden Way Publishing, 1993.

Trees That Please, 3084 Highway 47, Las Lunas, NM 87031, **866-**5027. This nursery offers trees grafted onto root stock suited to New Mexico's climates and alkaline soil.

▣ ▣ ▣

HOW TO GROW OAKS
IN DRY LANDS

A beautiful, well-placed tree can set the entire tone for a garden. So much the better if it also adapts well to our natural cycles of rain and drought. A seldom-planted but excellent tree that fulfills these requirements is the oak.

All oak lovers should visit the Trees That Please Tomé Nursery in Los Lunas. There, owner Michael Melendrez will show off his extensive selection of oaks, as well as many other southwest plants, while sharing his knowledge and expertise about these special trees.

Melendrez travels all over the state seeking the most magnificent, hardy and healthy specimens. From these trees he gathers acorns and carefully plants them, encouraging a well-branched root system for optimum growth.

Among the 26 varieties of oaks he offers, almost half of which are native to New Mexico, you'll find seedlings destined to become dainty patio trees, windbreaks, shade trees, or trees worthy of passing on to the grandchildren. Though Melendrez has not been at this long enough to offer any full-sized trees, his seedlings (up to 15 gallons) are affordable, adapt more easily than large trees to transplanting, and, if treated right, will grow quickly enough to satisfy the most impatient gardener.

Local Oak Myths

Why then, if native oaks have so many virtues, aren't they planted more often? Because they are victims of some persistent misconceptions, which Melendrez is delighted to disprove. Many people believe New Mexico's oaks are all shrubby runts, five to ten feet tall. Wrong. Many grow from 20 to 40 feet tall, some over 80 feet. For instance, one of the largest true Gambel's oaks (there are nine closely related species often mistakenly sold as Gambel's) stands 47 feet tall in Gila National Forest. Its trunk measures 18 feet around, and it has a crown spread of 85 feet. That's no shrub.

Another myth is that all oaks grow at a snail's pace. But at the Trees That Please test plots, there are varieties that grow from two to six feet per year. And even if you don't have such luck in your yard, many oaks will certainly outgrow the piñon (six inches a year) or the Rocky Mountain Juniper (eight inches a year).

Oaks, the Clever Survivors

In the wild, oaks thrive despite months of intense heat and drought. What are their survival strategies? First, some botanists speculate that oaks evolved a most unique adaptation to protect against fire danger. A specialized system of "sap" roots brings up water from deep underground, and releases it just below the soil surface. Would you believe a tree that waters itself? Melendrez believes most oaks have sap roots.

Though one botanist I spoke to referred to sap roots as "a nice theory," he admitted that the fact that most oaks withstand fire or are able to quickly regenerate suggests their ability to draw on deep water reserves.

Oaks have another advantage: Their roots encourage mycelial (fungal) growth in the soil—one of the most critical elements in a healthy ecosystem. Apparently, this growth is promoted by the natural acidity of layers of oak leaves as they break down. Fungi help the soil stay moist and produce food for plants they associate with, thus reducing stress.

Seven Ways to Help Your Oak Thrive

• Plant early in the fall. Temperatures are on their way down, yet the earth is still warm. Trees respond to these ideal conditions by growing lots of roots, until the ground freezes solid. More roots in fall result in vigorous growth later.

• Make the surrounding soil an attractive place for roots to enter. Loosen soil at least as wide as the tree is tall. Make sure the sides and bottom of the hole can be easily permeated by water and roots. (Eventually, lateral roots reach outwards the same number of feet as the tree is tall.)

• Mulch heavily with compost, extending it a foot or so past the planting hole. This prevents dry surrounding soil from wicking water away from the soil around the tree. Thick mulch also buffers temperature extremes which can kill root hairs, hampering the tree's progress. "Cap" the mulch (e.g., with straw, bark chips) so moisture remains in the soil.

• Plant these tough trees directly in the native soil, without compost or fertilizers mixed in. They'll venture into the neighboring soil much more quickly. If soils are extremely alkaline (like soil around new construction), add soil sulfur. Gypsum may be the ticket for highly salted alluvial soils.

• Whenever available, tuck fallen oak leaves under the mulch. Yard leaves or pine needles can also be added (no cottonwood leaves—they're alkaline).

• Irrigate at the edges of the root ball, twice a month in fall, then once a month throughout winter on a warm morning. Each year, extend both the irrigation and the mulch outwards, as the tree grows.

• Once fully established, most people agree our native oaks should not need much supplemental watering. But to imitate the slightly higher rainfall conditions where oaks are generally found, consider planting where the tree will receive extra runoff.

Trees That Please offers several oaks especially worth checking out: In the fast-growing, drought-tolerant category, try "El Capitan" (a Chinquapin oak), "Burnella" (a bur oak/shrub live oak hybrid about 30 feet tall), or the Texas post oak.

If it's sweet and nourishing acorns you're after, try "Caprock," the Emory oak, "El Capitan" or "Burnella." These varieties require a partner to produce fruit.

So do plant a few oaks (or better yet, an oak grove). They're resilient, water-thrifty, and add an important element of diversity to the garden ecosystem.

RESOURCES

Trees That Please Nursery, 3084 Highway 47, Los Lunas, NM 87031, 866-5027. Proprietor and oak wizard Michael Melendrez can help you satisfy all your oak fantasies.

Stalking the Wild Asparagus, Euell Gibbons, Alan C. Hood Publishing, Brattleboro, VT, 1987. Learn modern ways of preparing this ancient food: recipes for candied acorns, acorn bread and more.

❧ ❧ ❧

HOW TO HARVEST
FRESH VEGETABLES YEAR ROUND
(without building a greenhouse)

Do you dream of living someplace where you could grow vegetables all year? Short of moving to Hawaii, the next best solution is to explore the world of season extension. Here are some simple strategies to keep you munching home-grown vegetables long after other gardens are put to bed for the winter.

May 15 to October 15 is usually considered the "growing season" in Northern New Mexico—a brief five months. It really means that summer favorites like tomatoes, squash, melons, corn, beans, etc., can survive and thrive outdoors only between those two dates. These plants are sensitive to frost and require long hours of sunlight and warmth to ripen.

But avid vegetable gardeners, interested in stretching the limits of the growing season, are out in early spring as soon as they can wedge a trowel into the ground, planting cold-hardy vegetables. Indeed, many folks plant their peas on St. Patrick's day, a good two months before the final frost date. Some root vegetables (carrots, radishes, turnips, beets, etc.) can also be seeded well before May 15. And greens such as parsley, lettuce, arugula, chard, kale and spinach *like* the cold and are unimpressed by frosts.

There's a down side to early spring planting, though. Cold, soggy soils can slow germination way down. Since most seeds need warmth to sprout, it helps to place old storm windows or clear plastic over the soil a couple of weeks before you intend to plant.

The Mellow Fall Garden

If spring finds you too busy or you'd rather stay inside until the wind stops howling, don't worry. Just join the gardeners who tweak the limits of the other end of the growing season. They sow the same cold-tolerant vegetables again in July and August. Seeds sprout easily in the still-warm soil and mature in forgiving, cool fall weather. (An added benefit of the fall garden is that there are much fewer insects.)

You can actually store some fall-planted vegetables in the ground for later harvest—beets, carrots, kale, leeks, lettuce and other hardy greens. Mark their location, cover generously with straw, then enjoy the fall harvest. In the coldest months, the greens will go dormant, then begin growing again in March. (You'll be eating kale when your neighbors are planting their seeds.) For many root vegetables, most notably carrots and parsnips, the colder the winter, the sweeter the taste. You can harvest roots all winter.

The Cold Frame

Probably the most underrated and little used strategy for extending the growing season is the "cold frame." (This term is a misnomer, since the temperature inside it ranges from a little to a whole lot warmer than outside.) Its main use is to protect plants from freezing rains and heat-robbing winds. Thus, when fall crops (the greens work the best) are planted directly in the frame during late summer, the gardener can look forward to a winter harvest. Yes folks, that means January.

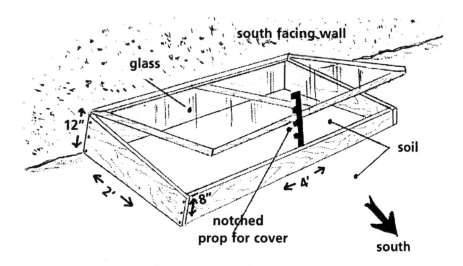

One version of a cold frame. Place the long dimension from east to west. You can take advantage of the warmth held in a south-facing wall or insulate the outside walls of the box with soil, straw or Styrofoam.

A cold frame is essentially a bottomless box which sits directly on the soil, with a see-through top (called "the light"). It can be any size, but the most manageable dimensions are two feet by four feet. The front wall is shorter than the rear wall so the sun's low rays can enter the box.

Walls are usually made of wood. Though you can make a fine cold frame out of straw bales, be aware the mice may think you've provided them not only shelter, but food, too! Leave wood unfinished and unsealed. To prevent the frame from rotting, attach strips of scrap wood about one inch thick to the bottom edge where it touches the soil. When the strips begin to rot in several years, replace them.

Construct the "light" (top) out of old wood frame storm windows, poly-carbonate or clear plastic stapled onto a simple wooden frame. If you choose plastic, wrap it around front and back to create a dead air space. Remove or prop the light open to harvest, and to allow heat to escape on sunny days.

Another option simpler than building a wooden cold frame is to drape beds (seeded by Labor Day) with one or two layers of a high quality row cover (*see* Resources), held off the plants by hoops. I've seen a very successful example of this using 3/8" rebar, covered with half-inch drip tubing to keep the cloth from tearing. Secure the row covers with rocks on the sides of the bed. On cold nights, cover with a tarp.

Beyond Winter Salads

But cold frames are not just for winter salads. They are useful all year long and can be moved to any location in the garden. Here are some examples:

• Use as a protected nursery for starting early spring seedlings.
• Give yourself a winter treat—grow pansies, violets and hardy bulbs.
• Use as a transition zone as you move small seedlings from indoors to outdoors.
•Take off the light in the summer, and cover with shade cloth to prevent spinach and lettuce from going to seed (and turning bitter).

So you see, with a little planning, you'll be ready for a four-season harvest.

RESOURCES

For a successful cold frame adventure, consult any of these resources:

Four Season Harvest, Eliot Coleman, Chelsea Green Publishing Co., Post Mills, VT, 1992. Coleman harvests his vegetables during freezing Maine winters. Complete planting schedules and instructions for cold frames and other strategies. Check out Coleman's excellent new update, *Farming the Back Side of the Calendar*, $15 postpaid from Four Season Farm, RR Box 14,

Harborside, ME 04642.

Square Foot Gardening, Mel Bartholomew, Rodale Press, Emmaus, PA, 1981. Bartholomew calls his versatile version of the cold frame a "sun box." A simple approach.

"Straw Bale Cold Frame," article in *Permaculture Drylands Journal*, Issue 18, Winter '92 - '93. Send $6.00 to PDJ, P.O. Box 156, Santa Fe, NM 87504-0156

The Cook's Garden catalogue **800-457-9703** Includes the regular cast of garden characters as well as many of the traditional European cool-season greens such as sorrel, mâche, endive, escarole, etc.

Peaceful Valley Farm Supply, P.O. Box 2209, Grass Valley, CA 95945, (888) 784-1722, offers an ingenious non-electric, adjustable, automatic open-er for the cold frame which is controlled with heat-sensitive paraffin.

Row covers: There are many available. The best I've seen is N-Sulate, a durable, spun polypropylene fabric which admits 70% sunlight, helps retain heat and moisture, and gives good wind protection. Contact Len Meserve, **466-1041**.

◉ ◉ ◉

PLANNING A MORE PRODUCTIVE VEGETABLE GARDEN

W ant to harvest more food from your garden this year? Thoughtful planning of the entire season (and I mean early spring all the way through fall) will help you do it. Here are some things to consider.

While all northern New Mexico communities have similar weather (gen-erally dry, lots of sun, cool nights, etc.), there are marked variations in the details. Of greatest importance to gardeners are the dates of the last spring and first fall frosts. (Some plants will expire if exposed to frost.) Ask the nurs-ery or call the County Cooperative Extension to learn the dates for your community. Be aware that nature is capricious, and the dates are approxima-tions at best. Nevertheless, you will be using these dates all year long to time your plantings.

Experiment With New Varieties

Northern New Mexico's growing season isn't particularly long, but it's certainly adequate to raise vegetables, as long as plant varieties are carefully chosen. Check the seed racks at your nursery, but please don't stop at that. There are some terrific catalogues (*see* Resources) which offer seeds for plants truly suited to our conditions.

Look for varieties that don't mind heat, drought, high altitude and/or short seasons. The description "dependable in the north" always catches my attention. "Early" varieties mature in fewer days than regular varieties. That's one reason I like to look at catalogues from Maine or Vermont—they offer seed for plants which do well in short seasons.

Do get out of the broccoli/squash/tomato/cucumber rut, and include some new vegetables this year. Mâche is a small-leafed, gourmet salad green with lots of names (corn salad, lamb's lettuce, field salad, fetticus). Eliot Coleman, Maine market gardener and author of *Four Season Harvest*, declares, "Mâche is so hardy, it could grow on an iceberg." I can vouch for that; as of January 14, mine looks fresh as spring under its straw mulch. It doesn't grow actively during winter, but it's there for the harvest.

Tatsoi, an oriental green, is incredibly hardy in the fall garden. It has a mild taste, good raw or cooked. I've also been impressed with Tyfon Holland greens (available only through Nichols Garden Nursery catalogue), dependable in spring and fall.

For the summer, try orach, a relative of cool-weather spinach, which loves to produce in hot weather. It's a quickie, ready to eat in just 30 days. Two lettuces that take the heat without bolting (going to seed and turning bitter) are Little Gem and Black-seeded Simpson.

And why not learn to grow grains? How about "multi-hued" quinoa, an ancient, nutritious Andean staple? All these and more await you in the catalogues.

Growing Cool-Season Crops

Spring and fall are like mirror images of each other, and cool-season crops can be grown in either season. In spring, seeds must germinate in cold soil. Most of them will, but it takes longer than in warm soil. Though some spring crops (like carrots and collards) can tolerate hot weather, most must mature before the full heat of summer. Since summer here tends to come on fast, you can see the importance of quick-maturing varieties and good timing.

Peas go into the garden the earliest—as much as two months before the last spring frost. Six to seven weeks before the last spring frost, you can plant leafy greens and root crops (except potatoes). Then about two weeks later, plant carrots and seedlings of broccoli, cauliflower and cabbage.

For me, growing cool-season crops for *fall* harvest (rather than spring) is less tricky. Seeds germinate readily in the warm soil of mid-summer, become seedlings as days are shortening, then mature in forgiving, cool fall weather. In fact, many root vegetables and most leafy members of the cabbage family (kale, collards, etc.) need a frost to taste their best. Some can be heavily mulched and harvested from the ground until it freezes solid; others (like chard and kale) can actually "overwinter" and start growing again in early spring.

The hardest thing about the fall garden is remembering to plant it in the summer! Start thinking about it in June; begin planting in July. A couple of weeks after the summer solstice, put in broccoli seedlings. Then two or two and a half months before the fall frost, plant any of the cool-season greens and the root vegetables. From that time until one month before frost, spinach, radishes and mâche can be seeded, to mature in the coldest weeks of October and November.

Warm-Season Crops

These are the plants that won't tolerate frost at all, and need heat to mature—squash, cucumber, peppers, tomatoes, corn, melons, etc. We have the heat, but our high altitude makes for cool nights in late summer, and this can prevent adequate ripening. It often pays to search out early, short-season varieties.

Putting it All Together

To get the most out of your garden beds, use "succession planting," which means growing different crops, one after another, in the same space. After each harvest, always add compost (preferably homemade) before reseeding the next crop. Compost provides low levels of many nutrients and adds soil life. (Other nutrients such as phosphorus and potash may need to be replenished as well.)

But soil amendments are not enough. You must also consider the characteristics of what you're growing. John Jeavons, in *How to Grow More Vegetables (than you ever thought possible on less land than you can imagine)*, divides vegetables into three main categories:

• HEAVY FEEDERS (HF), which use a lot of nutrients, especially nitrogen (corn, tomatoes, eggplant, peppers, squash, all leafy greens)

• HEAVY GIVERS (HG), which add nitrogen to the soil (all legumes, peas and beans)

• LIGHT FEEDERS (LF), which don't have high needs for nitrogen (all root crops)

By rotating crops and avoiding repeated plantings of HFs, you can prevent soil deficiencies or a buildup of microorganisms which can cause disease. (The one notable exception is tomatoes, which love to grow in the same spot for as many as five years in a row.)

Here are some sample rotations going from spring to fall:

BED #1: peas (HG)...tomatoes/squash (HF)...turnips (LF)

BED #2: leafy greens (HF)...potatoes (LF)...rutabagas/beets (LF)

BED #3: carrots/radishes/turnips (LF)...beans (HG)...broccoli (HF)
(For more information, see Jeavons' book or Eliot Coleman's *The New Organic Grower.*)

Other strategies for getting more food from your garden involve optimizing the use of space. You can interplant crops which mature at different times and have different root profiles, so they don't compete (e.g., lettuce+carrots+radishes). Or plant nitrogen-giving legumes in the same bed with the nutrient hogs (e.g., peas+arugula, beans+orach). The classic southwest example of this cooperative plan is combining beans, squash and corn—"the three sisters." The beans feed the squash and corn, the squash shades the ground for all three, and the corn provides a trellis to support the beans. Neat.

I don't mean to make all this sound simple—it isn't. But if you incorporate a few of these practices each year, I know your harvests will grow.

RESOURCES
Here are my favorite seed catalogues. Get them all; you won't be sorry.

Bountiful Gardens (707) 459-6410
Seeds of Change (888) 762-7333
Native Seeds/SEARCH (505) 268-9233
Seeds West (505) 843-9713
Ronniger's Seed & Potato Co. (800) 846-6178
Johnny's Selected Seeds (207) 437-4301
Fedco Seeds P.O. Box 520, Waterville, ME 04903-0520
Nichols Garden Nursery (541) 928-9280
The Cook's Garden (800) 457-9703

◆ ◆ ◆

Warding Off the Wind:
A PRIMER ON WINDBREAKS

Although a cool breeze on a summer evening is pleasant, the occasionally merciless spring winds of northern New Mexico can test our psyches, dry out soils and gardens, and remove topsoil. A carefully planned windbreak can cut down water loss from plants and soils by one third, as well as stop erosion. Oh yes, and preserve sanity.

There are endless variations of windbreaks planted worldwide. They divert, lift up, exhaust and otherwise confuse the wind, creating a relatively calm oasis for living and gardening. Windbreaks are commonly composed of a line (or several rows) of trees and shrubs, or a tall hedge placed perpendicular to the direction of prevailing winds.

Windbreaks for All Seasons

If you're born to grow vegetables, you'll be glad to hear that wind shelter increases spring, summer and fall garden yields, especially in taller crops like corn. A windbreak is also a boon for fruit trees, which are sensitive to hot, dry winds (they tend to drop their fruit).

If winter energy efficiency is your concern, place windbreaks to reduce cold air infiltration through the walls. Windbreaks reduce wind-carried summer heat as well.

How to Make Big Windbreaks

Don't grab your shovel until you understand how wind behaves around your house. Then, consider these three factors:

• **Length**: Because wind travels around the edges of a windbreak and eventually meets again in the middle, the row of plants must be longer than the area you want to protect.

• **Density**: Though it seems the most effective windbreak would be an impermeable wall, it's not. Wind whips over walls with renewed vigor and turbulence. Aim instead for a living wall of plants with about 65% density (some sources recommend up to 85%). This means as you look through it, you see only 35% of what's beyond it. The goal is a continuous but permeable barrier.

Density can be accomplished in three ways: use plants which have thick foliage (e.g., junipers, pines, etc.); plant several rows of plants with graduated

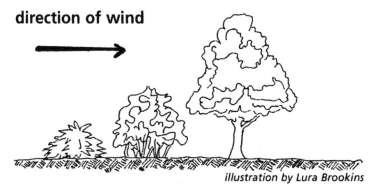

direction of wind

illustration by Lura Brookins

gradually stepped-up height of an effective windbreak

heights (shortest shrubs on windward side) and varying densities (*see* illustration); or use one row of trees/shrubs planted very closely together in a zig-zag or sinuous line.

• **Height**: The height of the tallest trees (at maturity) determines how far wind protection extends on the leeward side. Though many factors contribute to this distance of effectiveness, it's safe to say that a well-constructed windbreak with 65% or greater density will result in shelter for a distance from two to five times the height of the tallest trees. Wind speed will be reduced 60% to 80%. That means if your tallest trees are 25 feet, a 25 mile per hour wind will be slowed to 5 to 10 miles per hour, within an area from 50 to 125 feet on the leeward side of the break. (Lesser effects can be seen for a much greater distance.)

Little Breaks

Permanent respite for a small vegetable garden can be accomplished with a shrubby hedge, trellises with vines, or even an extra thick patch of Jerusalem artichokes. Again, make any windbreak slightly longer than the area needing protection. You can also construct temporary wind relief for sensitive plants while they're getting established. Woven mats staked in place, straw bales, or stick and brush fences all work well.

Great Plants for Windbreaks

Windbreak plants face lots of adversity, so be sure to choose plants that are up to the task. Lucky for us, we have scads of beautiful, water thrifty, wind tolerant plants, well adapted to and eager to grow in poor soils. What's more, many of our native shrubs provide chow and habitat for wild birds. (You can eat what the birds don't.)

Listed are approximate ranges of mature heights for three groups of plants—check nurseries and plant catalogues for specific information.

Shrubs 3 to 6 feet tall
    Apache Plume (N)*
    Four Wing Saltbush*
    Three Leaf Sumac*
    Western Sandcherry
    Big Sage
Shrubs/shrubby trees 6 to 15 feet tall
    Native Plum*
    New Mexico Privet*
    Fernbush
    Mountain Mahogany (N)

Siberian Peashrub (N)
Autumn Olive (N)
Sea Buckthorn (N)

Trees 15 to over 30 feet tall
Eastern Redcedar*
New Mexico Locust (N)*
Purple Robe Locust (N)
Gambel Oak*
Austrian Pine*
Rocky Mountain Juniper*
Arizona Cypress (Nursery cultivars "Blue Pyramid" or "Blue Ice" have
    better survival rates than other Arizona Cypress trees.)
available as seedlings from New Mexico State Forestry
(N) manufactures nitrogen for soil

Both wind and fire gain speed as they travel up slopes. If you live at or near the top of a slope (or worse, a ridge), your windbreak should consist of fire-resistant plants. Seek help from a knowledgeable landscape designer.

Planting Tips

Nature abhors straight lines (as well as vacuums), so plant in sinuous or zig-zag lines. The Forestry Division suggests planting seedlings in an area which concentrates runoff water, and in conjunction with weed barrier cloth and/or mulch (four to six inches of shredded bark, straw, etc.). By covering the ground at least three feet around plants, water is held in the soil, and weeds which compete with seedlings for available water are suppressed.

Plant into wide areas of loosened native soil, *without* rich soil amendments, fertilizer, compost, etc. Instant gratification isn't part of the windbreak planting experience, but these steps will help your long term investment to grow as fast as it can.

Remember, plants grow out to the side as well as up. Though opinions vary on plant spacing, here are some guidelines: In a multiple row windbreak, plant shrubs no closer to each other than three feet, medium trees no closer than eight feet, tall trees no closer than 10 feet. Between the rows of shrubs and trees, allow 12 feet or more. In a single row windbreak, plants might be squeezed a bit closer together.

But What Do They Cost?

Anyone who's checked prices of full grown nursery stock is probably wondering how it's possible to plant a windbreak and stay out of debt. Costs for a

70 foot windbreak (seven large trees, eight medium trees and nine shrubs) might set you back around $2,000. Which brings me to the many advantages of seedlings and immature plants. That same windbreak would run between $50 and $100 for Forestry seedlings, or perhaps $450 for young plants from a nursery. The larger the nursery plant, the more cramped (or absent) its roots are, and the harder for it to adapt under adverse conditions. Small seedlings can and will catch up to larger plants, sometimes startlingly quickly.

They say that the best time to plant a windbreak is 20 years ago...it's true. It's also true that time flies. Start planning your windbreak today.

RESOURCES

New Mexico Forestry & Resources Conservation Division, P.O. Box 1948, Santa Fe, NM 87504-1948, 476-3325. To order windbreak seedlings from the Forestry, you must own at least one acre of land in New Mexico. For advice on successful tree planting techniques, and dates for workshops, contact Kim Kostelnik in Santa Fe.

Bear Creek Nursery, P.O. Box 411, Northport, WA 99157, (509) 732-6219, offers an incredible variety of bare root seedlings at excellent prices. They have conservation grade stocks, edible perennials, all kinds of fruit and nut trees, plants appropriate for windbreaks, etc.

Introduction to Permaculture, by Bill Mollison with Reny Mia Slay, Tagari Publications, New South Wales, 1991. Windbreaks are explained on pages 45 to 50.

◈ ◈ ◈

AN INTRODUCTION TO PERMACULTURE

Atruly natural garden, when mature, works like a healthy ecosystem, providing for its own needs and recycling its own wastes, with a minimum of intervention by the gardener. It should not require large inputs of labor, money, gadgets, chemicals, or much use of machinery. Thus, the gardener is free to wander about, nibbling on raspberries, admiring the fall colors and assessing the garden's progress. Sounds good, doesn't it?

Regardless of the scope of your project, or whether you live in the city or the country, permaculture can help you achieve this goal by offering direction in sensible earthcare. What's more, the resulting garden designs are frequently beautiful.

So What Is Permaculture?

The word permaculture is a combination of "permanent/agriculture" or "permanent/culture," and is a term coined by Australian Bill Mollison more than 20 years ago.

An extended study of forests, oceans and farming practices of indigenous cultures worldwide nourished the vision of permaculture. Mollison recalls, "In 1974, I was able to articulate what permaculture was. It was pretty simple. It was that we can construct plant and animal systems that not only support themselves (for reproduction, maintenance and growth), but also feed us."

Don't think it's just about small-scale farming, though. Even if you're not hankering to grow your own potatoes or raise chickens, permaculture has a lot to offer. Permaculture, for instance, is much more than just a collection of techniques. It's also a philosophy, a set of ethics, and a way of seeing. (Permaculture later broadened to include strategies for access to land and innovative business and financial planning—but that's another article.)

The Land Reveals All

The first step in creating a permaculture garden—prolonged observation —is often overlooked. Indeed, it's best to live with a garden or a piece of land for four seasons before taking action. As you observe, consider these important points:

• Where does water go as it leaves your roof or runs off other surfaces (driveway, patio, paths)? How does it behave as it moves across the land? Is there evidence of erosion or pooling? Go outside during the next rainstorm (and definitely during summer monsoons).

• Map the path of the sun in the winter and summer skies. Get to know where shady and sunny areas are, all year.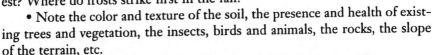

• From what direction(s) does the wind come? Where's the windiest spot? the calmest spot? the warmest? the coldest? Where do frosts strike first in the fall?

• Note the color and texture of the soil, the presence and health of existing trees and vegetation, the insects, birds and animals, the rocks, the slope of the terrain, etc.

• Where do people prefer to hang out, walk? Map your traffic patterns.

This is the beginning of the story of your landscape. If you ignore it, you're in danger of making decisions based on abstract theories (or worse, no theory at all) that ignore what really happens where you live. In order to harmonize with the wind, sun, rain and earth and gently lead them in the desired direction, you need to know how they behave. Only then will these powerful energies actually begin to work *for* you.

Make The Links

Now that you've gathered this information, the next step is to make connections between your needs (e.g., plants or food you want to grow, more shade, desire to conserve water, ways you want to enjoy your garden) and the activities, structures, resources and natural forces present on your land. Bring an uninhibited imagination to this task.

Each element (such as a pathway, a storage shed, the compost pile, a fruit tree, the vegetable patch) is placed in relationship to other elements so that they support one another. In good designs, each need is supported by at least two or three elements, and each major element provides for several different needs. Here's how it works:

• A need, such as a desire to conserve water, could be supported by the following elements: collect rain water off the roof into cisterns, choose drought-tolerant native plants, mulch everything, grow vegetables in sunken beds or alongside flagstone paths that shed water, use windbreaks to slow drying winds, collect water in catchments before it runs off slopes.

• An element such as a carefully constructed windbreak could provide for many needs. In addition to breaking up and dispersing wind, it might afford privacy, feed the family, shade plants grown underneath it, furnish mulch or compost materials, protect against fire, supply wildlife food and habitat, prevent erosion, draw "beneficial" insects (which feed on "pest" insects), etc.

It gets really interesting when an element considered to be a waste product or a "problem" (weeds, for instance) is suddenly seen as a positive thing. I welcome all the purslane, spurge and wild amaranth that have shown up on bare spots on my windblown land. The roots of these weeds hold the soil and keep it from eroding. I'll gather blue grama grass seed, so abundant since the summer rains, and throw it in among the weeds. There it may find enough shelter to stick around until spring, when it can sprout. Without the weeds, the seeds would blow away. And grama grass, being a perennial, will eventually choke out the weeds, which are annuals. No cost, little labor, good result.

You'll feel clever, too, when you realize a use for some newly generated "resource." How about the large rocks you removed from the new vegetable bed? Why not use them to build a loose rock wall giving temporary protection for those seedlings you just planted on the windy side of the house? The rock shelter also offers housing for insect-eating lizards and a perch for birds who deposit their phosphorus-rich manure. (Bird droppings often contain wildflower seeds, conveniently packaged—no extra charge.)

The possibilities are endless ....

• Need more space to raise food? Compost part of your lawn and turn it into an edible landscape next spring.

• Group different types of plants together so they feed (some plants give nitrogen to the soil as they grow), shelter and protect one another. Add in plants that draw beneficial insects and you have a whole system that is greater than the sum of its parts.

• Use off-site (usually free) waste products to enrich your site. Collect manure from local stables, shredded bark (available at some landfill sites) to use for soft pathways, straw from straw-bale building construction sites, damaged produce discarded by markets for your compost pile, bags of leaves and other yard waste from local gardeners. You'll never buy compost again.

Begin to see everything (including problems) as a potential resource; search for how things could connect. The more connections, the stronger and more resilient your garden ecosystem becomes. This is permaculture. Well, actually, this is only a fraction of what permaculture is, but it should still give you something to think about.

What I've Gained from Permaculture

By looking at my landscape through the filter of permaculture philosophy, I've found dramas and insights as profound as if I had gone on a vision quest. Most valuable to me is a new attitude toward nature—one of greater trust, imagination, playful exploration, and a feeling of partnership.

Permaculture challenges me to learn a unique way of seeing. I am asked to abandon the usual narrowly-focused, problem-oriented approach and look instead at the whole system. Sometimes solutions are the opposite of what I expect. Bill Mollison once said to a student, "You don't have a grasshopper problem, you have a duck deficiency!"

I see permaculture as a tool for the evolution of a garden which is not only attractive but has the potential to be productive, resource-conserving, self-sustaining, and a source of personal growth and pleasure.

RESOURCES

Introduction to Permaculture, by Bill Mollison with Reny Mia Slay, Tagari Publications, Australia, 1991. Packed with useful information for your permaculture adventures.

URBAN Permaculture: A Practical Handbook for Sustainable Living, by David Watkins, Permaculture Resources Inc., Califon, NJ, 1993. Offers ways to apply a permaculture approach to any homestead, with or without access to open land.

Permaculture Drylands Journal: Back issues of this informative journal are available. Write P.O. Box 156, Santa Fe, NM 87504-0156, 983-0663. Basic and advanced training courses are offered in Santa Fe, Albuquerque, Taos, and other locations in the southwest. For information about courses, call the **Permaculture Drylands Institute**, 983-0663. The permaculture contact in Taos is Brigid Meier, 758-1318. For information about Albuquerque courses, call the Albuquerque Permaculture Guild Hotline, 281-4871.

Check out this web site: **www.permaculture.net**

EcoVersity, 2639 Agua Fria, Santa Fe, offers courses in Permaculture. *www.ecoversity.org*

PART 2:

Herbs and Weeds

WHY IT PAYS TO MAKE FRIENDS WITH WEEDS

Weeds are sweated over, assaulted with chemicals, considered by most as the curse of the gardener, useless at best. But these much-maligned innocents are less intrinsically diabolical than they are thoroughly misunderstood. Sure, there are a few mighty troublesome plants, but many weeds can help your garden thrive, feed you, heal you—or all three. I know it may seem curious at first glance, but weeds occupy an honored place in the natural order of whole systems.

Weeds are like the doctors in troubled ecosystems. Some seek out sad, depleted soil and send strong roots deep into the subsoil. There they draw out and stash in their leaves new materials—potassium, calcium, phosphorus, trace minerals. Then, they donate their lives to the cause of enriched topsoil. (Another great place for them to rot is in your compost pile. What a pity so many end up improving soil at the landfill.)

Sometimes, their mission is to protect bare or disturbed ground. As annual weeds decompose, they leave behind humus and more porous soil, setting the stage for other plants to prosper. Weeds are nature's disaster plan, par excellence. Only if land is completely denuded by erosion or killed by chemicals will there be no weeds—not exactly cause for rejoicing.

Their untamed genetic qualities make them resilient in harsh climates, and resistant to bug problems. Periodically, plant breeders resort to weeds to strengthen our "improved" pampered cultivars. Knowledgeable farmers used to "read weeds" like oracles, for indications of changes in the quality, fertility and drainage of their fields. And some weeds, because of their beneficial influences, were even grown intentionally with crops. For instance, amaranth (sometimes called pigweed) helps potatoes, peppers, eggplant, tomatoes, onions and corn to flourish. Sow thistle works similarly.

Good Credentials

With such good credentials, it's no surprise that weeds make superior chow and medicines. Each weed excels in at least one nutrient—some in many. Mallow (*Malva neglecta*, "cheeseweed") makes a yummy, hearty boiled green. A three-ounce serving contains more iron than beef liver and is high in calcium and beta carotene. Mallow's dried leaves make a mineral-rich tea, and a fresh leaf poultice soothes inflammation. Its small, nutritious seeds, which resemble tiny rounds of French cheese, have a nutty taste. Many adults may remember feasting on these "cheeses" as children.

Lambs quarters provide almost three times the calcium of an equal amount of milk, and offer a better balance of co-factors magnesium and phosphorus. Cook them like spinach. Raw, the leaves can form the basis of a unique and colorful wild salad mix—just add purslane, amaranth leaves, sorrel, nasturtium and edible flowers (Johnny jump-ups, rose petals, bachelor buttons, etc.).

Look a little further, you'll find more. Amaranth was once a staple in ancient cultures; a wild variety is surely lurking in your yard. Edible leaves, raw or cooked, and high-quality protein in the seeds are its claim to fame. Purslane adds a hint of lemony flavor to salads and soups. It's particularly rich in essential fatty acids (like the Omega 3s which cost megabucks at your nearest health food store). Cut your cholesterol and boost your immune system—for free.

What about the common dandelion (*Taraxacum officinale*, "official remedy for disorders")? With a botanical name like that, shouldn't you be raising some? The fresh greens (with almost twice the beta carotene as spinach) are great sautéed with garlic and olive oil. Dandelion root tea gives sluggish livers a gentle push, and the dried leaves make a diuretic tea which won't deplete potassium like many drugs will. I could go on. There are so many amazing weeds. Imagine if folks with marginal food budgets (and nutrition) regained the simple skills of wild food harvesting taken for granted a couple of generations ago.

When to Hoe

All well and good, but let's say you've inherited a neglected yard, and you're wondering how to manage your weed bonanza. I mean, how much tumbleweed can one person eat? (You guessed it. When they're about three inches high, tumbleweeds are nutritious and edible, though this side of bland.) Timing is of the essence when removing weeds. Of course, they're easiest to pull after a rain. Don't use a hoe to cut weeds off at the ground before they flower or begin seed formation, or they'll simply try again, much harder. The best time for hoeing annuals is just before seeds mature. After a good rain, it's easy to pull out many perennials (whole root attached, please). If you despise pulling them, contribute to the local economy: hire neighborhood kids. If it's too late and they've already gone to seed, your best bet is "sheet mulching" (*see* page 11-12) which results in rich soil six months later. Permanently, thickly mulched yards don't suffer many weeds. The cardinal rule: Don't let unwanted weeds spread their seeds.

Do plant or mulch cleared spaces; mother nature recolonizes bare ground with more weeds. You can bake weeds under clear or black plastic (this does kill friendly soil bacteria, however), or subdue them with a heavy thatch of straw. I heard about pouring white vinegar on weeds, and tried it on the young tumbleweeds on my driveway: they died. Weeds between flagstones and bricks succumb to a boiling water bath. Timing is critical: most germination occurs in April, May, September and October, so get them while they're young and vulnerable.

Check out "Weed Aside" (made from vegetable oils), which dehydrates young weeds when applied in warm, dry weather; and "Wow Plus!" or "Original Wow!" (basically corn gluten), which inhibits roots of weed seedlings from sprouting in lawns and flower beds. Both are simple, eminently safe products.

Poisoning weeds with herbicides is a whole different game, played by thousands across the country. The brand names sound actually playful: Roundup, Weed-Be-Gon. The nasty truth is these poisons are *not* fully degraded in the soil, and *do* have serious cumulative health consequences. They often end up many miles from their point of use, in water, food, birds and you. (Do read the revealing *Consumer Reports* article, "Greener greens? The truth about organic food," January, 1998.) According to the Environmental Protection Agency, most herbicides are more toxic than insecticides. The list of weed enemies on the container reads like a wild foods supermarket and natural medicine chest, causing wild food enthusiasts and herbalists to cringe.

Now, what do you think? I'll bet the next time you see your neighbor going nearly mad over the dandelions in his lawn, you'll have a few things to say. In the meantime, bon appetit.

RESOURCES

Weeds of the West, Tom Whitson, Ed., Western Society of Weed Science, Newark, CA 1992. The clearest photos I've ever seen, of just about every common weed. Consult a copy at your local nursery.

Stalking the Wild Asparagus, Euell Gibbons, Alan C. Hood Publishing,

Brattleboro, 1987. First published in 1962, and still a classic.

Gardens Alive! (513) 354-1482, www.gardensalive.com. Source for Wow Plus! and Weed Aside.

Seeds of Change, P.O. Box 15700, Santa Fe, NM 87506-5700 (888) 762-7333. If you don't have the patience for the right weeds to show up in your yard, order some! Certified organic (cultivated, not wild) amaranth, dandelion and lambs quarters seeds. Heirloom varieties with large, succulent leaves, good seed production, etc.

IMPORTANT NOTE: Do not pick and eat unknown plants. Check with an experienced forager for positive identification and other safety factors involved.

❦ ❦ ❦

GROWING A BACKYARD MEDICINE CHEST GARDEN

If you long for more connection with nature, growing your own plant medicines is an exquisite way to get sewn in for keeps. Using herbs is a feast for the senses, a balm for the spirit, and a great way to become more self-sufficient.

Minor ailments respond quickly to the simplest of remedies. So here are five ordinary plants full of heart and soul: yarrow, chamomile, mullein, comfrey and peppermint. Among them, an astonishing 45 minor health problems can be addressed. That they work is proven by hundreds of years of usage (thousands for yarrow), and modern studies which confirm the ancient uses.

In the Garden

These five adaptable herbs take minimal care. In spring and fall, offer compost to the chamomile, comfrey and yarrow (skip the fertilizer). Making the soil too rich cuts down on production of the very oils that make these herbs work well.

Yarrow, a perennial, can be pushy, spreading by its creeping roots. Chamomile is an annual. As you collect the flowers, do leave some on the plant so it reseeds itself. Mullein, a biennial, forms a small rosette of leaves during its first year. The second year, its flowering stalk shoots up four to six feet. This sentry of the garden will grow in the most wretched soils, and needs no watering or feeding. Put it in full sun where you won't mind it spreading...which it will, vigorously, via *thousands* of tiny black seeds.

If you doubt your gardening abilities, grow comfrey and peppermint—

your thumbs will quickly turn green. Both are perennial, returning year after year with little effort on your part. Though they tolerate full sun, they'll appreciate some shade, and will need much less water that way. Mulch heavily around comfrey to cut down on water loss, and add compost and rotted manure in spring and fall. Once established, mint won't need much water. In tiny gardens, peppermint's relentless advances (via creeping roots) can be checked by placing it in a large flower pot (with drainage holes) buried in the ground.

A contented comfrey plant forms a deep, moist root and a prodigious amount of huge (rather bristly) leaves. If this 3-foot plant makes too big a statement in your garden, just keep harvesting older leaves—besides medicine, they make great mulch and are a boon to the compost pile. Beware moving comfrey to another location: Leave behind even a sliver of the root, and it starts up all over again. Prevent it from going to seed, and place it carefully, because it's doubtful you'll ever get rid of it. (Not recommended for the highly controlling gardener.)

The Herbs:
YARROW, *Achillea millefolium* (Spanish: plumajillo)

For your herb garden, you want this lacy, white-flowered variety, not the huge yarrow with yellow flowers commonly used in landscaping. Wilderness guides often name oak as the most useful first aid plant; I'm happier to find yarrow on my hikes, which has a dozen distinct uses.

Yarrow stops bleeding of minor cuts—crush or chew fresh leaves, apply as a poultice. It also prevents infection, speeds healing of tissue, and lessens inflammation and pain. Use fresh leaves on insect bites, too. Even a nosebleed can be halted by placing a fresh, bruised leaf inside the nostril. (I use a mixture of leaves *and* flowers for all the situations which follow.)

By promoting a sweat, a cup of hot yarrow tea reduces the heat of a dry fever. Did you know you can sweat out viruses along with other wastes? So use for incipient colds as well. What if your feverish child refuses the tea? A no-hassle way to get herbs into kids is by bathing them in herb teas. (If this stretches your belief too thin, consider that the late, great 20th century French herbalist Maurice Mességué got fabulous results using almost nothing *but* herbal hand and foot baths.)

Yarrow calms visceral spasms, whether due to gas, tension, or menstrual cramps: try the tea or a bath.

Though headaches have a multitude of possible causes, it's worth trying yarrow, which "moves" blood and energy. Besides, in your tea you'll also get an anti-inflammatory oil (azulene), salicylic acid (like Aspirin), and an anesthetic (eugenol). Not bad for a humble herb.

But what about yarrow's bitter taste? This despised flavor is studiously avoided in most American diets (did you eat your parsley garnish?). But bodies need *all* flavors to be healthy. In moderation, the bitter taste stimulates the flow of digestive juices, improves assimilation, and more. (You can't get the benefits by swallowing it in a capsule, since it works by a nerve reflex on the tongue. Sorry.)

Sipping a bitter tea will relieve stalled digestion due to emotional upset or occasional nausea after eating. In mere minutes, you'll feel your guts gearing up to return to action.

Drunk cool, yarrow tea increases the flow of urine and soothes the irritation and pain of a urinary tract infection.

GERMAN CHAMOMILE, *Matricaria recutita* or *M. chamomilla* (Spanish: manzanilla)

Botanists can't decide what to call this plant, so be sure you get German and not the more bitter Roman chamomile. This miniature daisy is particularly effective for peevish children with colic, teething pains, restlessness and such. It even calmed Peter Rabbit's unruliness.

Some of its talents are similar to yarrow: it's antiseptic, anti-inflammatory, aids digestion, and heals wounds and sores. I include it here because of its affinity to the nervous system and its more accessible flavor. Think of using it when problems are made worse by anxiety or sensitivity. Rich in the anti-inflammatory oil azulene, chamomile soothes whatever it touches, inside or out. Make a strong tea (1 Tablespoon per cup water) to calm spasms, protect against the formation of ulcers and help heal existing ones. If your gut is inflamed from the likes of stomach flu, combine with a pinch of peppermint leaves. Don't forget to try the tea as a mouthwash for sensitive gums or a gargle for sore throats.

I've seen a chamomile eyewash clear up irritation and discharge almost instantly.

MULLEIN, *Verbascum thapsus* (Spanish: gordo lobo, or punchón)

Though mullein leaves are more often used, few people know that the flowers are actually the stronger medicine. Gather both and see for yourself. (Flowers are available commercially only in oil form.) Extra sensitive folks should strain both flower and leaf teas through filter paper to remove fine hairs.

As tea, this friendly, fuzzy plant relaxes tight lungs, tones weepy mucous membranes, and decreases inflammation. Mullein is a "thinking herb"—it seems to know what to do, when. It increases fluid production if lungs are too dry, but brings up mucus if and when that's needed. Teasing coughs, persistent bronchitis, inflamed windpipe: all are helped by mullein tea.

Mullein excels in topical uses as well. The fresh leaves make an excellent poultice for shingles, boils and sores. I wouldn't be without the infused oil made from the flowers, a blessing for earaches: Store the oil in a dropper bottle, warm the bottle slightly, then place 2-3 drops in each ear and plug ears with cotton. (Caution: Never put *anything* in an ear which is draining.) Apply the oil also to hypersensitive skin due to neuritis or neuralgia, or dry, itchy ear canals.

COMFREY, *Symphytum officinale* (Spanish: consuelda)

Have you heard stories about the dangers of comfrey? While ingesting the root is generally not advised, topical use of the root or leaf poses no risk whatsoever. (The harmful substance in the root isn't well-absorbed through the skin.)

Though the root has a broader scope of action than the leaf, both heal and soothe inflammation. Comfrey leaf contains vitamin C, minerals, beta carotene and anti-oxidants—great nutrients for the skin. Leaf tea makes a nice sunburn spray or a bath for itchy, dry skin or diaper rash.

Comfrey root offers a slippery substance herbalists affectionately call mucilage. What's more, the root includes lots of allantoin, which promotes cell growth and speeds the mending of damaged tissue. Use powdered, dried root as an unrivaled, marvelously gooey poultice on stubborn skin ulcers, scrapes, chapped skin, etc. It prevents scarring, too. The root powder, when sprinkled directly on cuts, stops bleeding and forms an instant scab ... it's the Krazy Glue of the herb world.

Comfrey's Latin name, *Symphytum* ("to unite"), and its alias, "knitbone," describe the root's action on fractured bones. Try the poultice on hairline or uncasted fractures, sprains, slow-to-regenerate cartilage, and to reduce pain and swelling of injuries.

PEPPERMINT, *Mentha piperita* (Spanish: menta)

This herb, besides being a refreshing, fragrant beverage tea, can be used like yarrow for mild headaches, colds and fevers. But it's peppermint's ability to cool and anesthetize which wins it a place in your medicine garden.

Containing appreciable amounts of menthol, a cup of strong peppermint tea chills out ragged stomach nerves and chases nausea. In fact, its soothing action extends throughout the gut, "settling" digestion, calming irritability, gas and cramping. For children, strong peppermint tea can be unpleasant— make theirs half-strength.

Peppermint provides welcome coolness for itchy, burned or bitten skin. Spray on a mist of the tea, or soak in a tepid mint bath. Make it brief, though; an extended bath can be more chilling than you'd want.

USER'S GUIDE

Gathering and Storing Your Harvest

First, some general rules: Don't pick wet herbs; don't dry or store herbs in direct sunlight. Every few mornings, pick mullein and chamomile flowers individually, place one layer thick in straw baskets lined with paper towel (or on screens). Large, second-year mullein leaves are cut off near the stalk, strung with needle and thread, and hung to dry. Gather comfrey leaves (wear gloves) mid-to-late summer, bundling them at their stems. When yarrow and mint bloom, clip the upper eight to 12 inches, group six to eight stalks in a bouquet, and rubber-band at the cut end. Hang herb bunches upside down out of the sun, where air circulates freely. Dig comfrey root after the first fall frost. (Return a piece to the soil.) Allow dirt to dry, then brush off (don't rinse). Chop into quarter-inch pieces, spread to dry one layer thick in baskets or on screens.

When herbs are bone-dry, break up minimally to fit into *dry* glass jars, discarding yarrow and mint stems. Grind one cup of dried comfrey root into powder (use electric spice grinder or blender), and leave the rest whole. Label and date the jars; replace in one year.

Making and Taking Medicines

General rules: Use glass, enamel or stainless steel only.

Tea ("infusion"): Boil one cup water. Add one to two teaspoons (smaller amount for children) of dried, crumbled herb (twice that amount of fresh herb), turn off heat, cover, and steep about 10 minutes. Dosage: Some intuition is needed here. Drink one-half to one cup, two to three times daily (half that for kids or elderly). If the problem doesn't resolve within a few days, see a practitioner.

Eyewash: Boil one cup purified water, add 1/4 teaspoon salt. Turn off heat, add one scant teaspoon desired herb. Cover, steep 10 minutes. *Strain through filter paper.* Wash eyes with warm solution using sterilized glass eyedropper or eyecup. Make a fresh batch of tea daily. Use three times daily for two days. (If any eye problem persists, see a doctor immediately.)

Herbal Bath: Boil two quarts water, place a rounded handful of dried herbs (twice that for fresh) into water, turn off heat. Cover, steep 20 minutes, strain into warm bath. Bathe one to two times daily for 15-20 minutes.

Poultice: Pound or bruise fresh herbs slightly, to awaken their powers. (Comfrey leaf is prickly — crush thoroughly.) If using dry herbs, crumble, moisten with boiled water. Add some comfrey root powder (or flour) to help herbs stick together. (A poultice entirely of comfrey root powder is best made by sprinkling the powder onto a tablespoon of water while stirring, not the other way around.) Oil unbroken skin to prevent sticking, place herbs on skin. Cover with a clean cloth, remove after 15 minutes. Use two times daily (or more) for two to three days.

Infused Oil: Fill a clean, *dry* two ounce glass jar with *fresh* herb or chopped fresh root and cover with olive oil. Stir with a chopstick to remove air bubbles. Cap loosely so air can escape, place in dark spot. Wait four to six weeks, then strain through filter paper. (Put a blotter of some kind under the jar, because strange as it may seem, the oil has a tendency to migrate out of the jar and down the sides.)

For Safety's Sake

Most herbs are safe because they are such complex biochemical compounds. Exerting a variety of effects at once, they buffer themselves. However, consult a professional herbalist before giving herbs to infants, pregnant or breast-feeding women, the frail elderly, and anyone with a serious medical condition. (Essential oils—extremely potent substances—are *not* used similarly to fresh or dried whole herbs.) Long-term treatment of chronic conditions is beyond the scope of this article; these suggestions are strictly for acute problems or flare-ups—doses are small, treatment is brief. Remember, overusing herbs can cause problems. When using any herb for the first time, use a small amount to make sure it agrees with you.

RESOURCES

When ordering or buying herbs, it's important to mention both common and Latin names, so you get the right plant. You'll find chamomile, comfrey, peppermint and yarrow at most nurseries, but not the preferred species of mullein (considered a weed).

J.L. Hudson, Seedsman, Star Rt 2, Box 337, La Honda, CA 94020, *www.jlhudsonseeds.com*

Elixir Farm Botanicals, Brixey, MO 65618, (417)261-2393, e-mail: efb@aristotle.net. For those interested in raising Chinese medicinal plants.

Johnny's Selected Seeds, 1 Foss Hill Road, RR 1 Box 2580, Albion, ME 04910-9731, (207) 437-4301. A wide selection of organic seeds of high quality, many produced on their own certified organic farm.

BOOK:

The New Age Herbalist, Richard Mabey, Macmillan Publishing Co., NY 1988. Despite its somewhat flaky title, this book has a solid core of responsible information, and explores every way you could think of to use herbs—vinegars, dyeing, healing, cosmetics, etc. The remarkably clear photographs are almost as good as being eyeball to eyeball with the herbs, except you can't smell them.

THE UNEXPECTED GIFTS OF STINGING NETTLE

Occasionally, Ma Nature comes up with an extraordinarily useful plant. Stinging nettle (*Urtica dioica*) is one such plant. Though it's feared, hated and underrated, every inch of the plant—root, leaf, stalk and seed—offers gifts. Learn to respect it, and it will go to work for you.

Nettle is often mistaken for a large mint, but a closer look reveals tiny hairs covering the leaves and stems. Brush lightly against the fresh plant (ouch!) and these hairs release skin irritants resulting in short-lived redness, a burning feeling and, though rarely, hives. So where's the gift?

Dyes, Nets, Wine and Cheese

Everywhere it grows, nettle has a long history of use. In addition to being valued as superior food and medicine, the plant formed part of the fabric of survival and cultural practices in many regions. Pounded stems yield strong fiber for fishing nets and cordage, as well as thread for a variety of fabrics—from fine, silky cloth to canvas. Leaves make a rich green dye, the roots a yellow dye. Tea acts like rennet, curdling milk in cheese making. Our forebears dined on nettle wine (or beer), and used concoctions made from the seeds to make their hair thick and sleek.

Nettle plays a dynamic role in the garden as well. The plant enlivens and conditions soil, speeds decomposition in compost heaps, and improves the health and vigor of plants. Just soak a handful of fresh nettle stalks (leaves attached) in a covered barrel of rainwater until it begins to ferment. Strain and use in a watering can or spray onto foliage.

Although nettle is most often found near streams, this highly adaptable plant can succeed in the drylands. Provide a northeast exposure, extra shade in June and July, and moderately rich, well-drained soil. Water deeply once or twice weekly. The creeping roots won't damage foundations or septic lines, but they may be hard to eradicate once established, so be sure of your placement.

For garden use, gather nettles any time. If you want to eat them or make medicine, collect before they set seed. Don't forget to dry some leaves for winter use. Now, about those stinging hairs: Just as cactus spines don't stop enterprising people from eating tasty prickly pears, nettle hairs can be dealt with. Leather gloves and long sleeves make gathering nettles a cinch. Dry or cook the leaves, and the hairs are disarmed. Dry as you would yarrow or mint (*see* page 64), then remove the leaves. Wear gloves, because the stems never lose their prickliness.

After the killing frost in the fall, cut nettles to the ground, and look forward to their return next spring. Do give something back to their soil (manure, compost or some cut nettles themselves), or eventually your nettle patch will sicken.

Real Food

For me, nettle satisfies an almost cellular hunger; eating it the first time each spring approaches a religious experience. It is one of the highest known sources of protein in a leafy green, and offers a broad palette of vitamins, minerals and micronutrients. Although nettle leaves are used exactly as you would spinach or chard, their rich, hearty flavor has much more pizzazz. They contain so much chlorophyll they nearly stain the pot green. (Indeed, leaves are used today as a commercial source of chlorophyll.) For the simplest preparation, simmer five minutes in a small amount of water; turn once during cooking. (I season mine with butter and tamari soy sauce.) Save the broth for a soup base, or savor it as a beverage.

Herbal Health Insurance

When nettle is used as fodder, chickens lay more eggs, cows produce more milk, and tired, drab horses become frisky and sport shinier coats. Is it surprising, then, that nettle does a few things for humans? This humble plant excels in an area modern pharmaceuticals can't touch—keeping things working well so they don't break down in the first place.

A restorative, tonifying herb, nettle vitalizes and normalizes glands and organs, purifies the blood and strengthens bones. In a paradoxical vein, juice or tea from *fresh* leaves soothes burns and stings—even nettle stings. Go figure. Though it increases nursing moms' milk, it is also astringent, stopping inappropriate bleeding, drying up waterlogged lungs, etc. An alcohol extract of *fresh* leaves helps relieve hay fever. Because nettle promotes excretion of excess acids, it's great for gouty, creaky joints and some skin conditions.

Regular use is like giving your body a new set of spark plugs. Of course, the best time for new plugs is after a lethargic winter of heavy foods. A mess of fresh nettle greens is the perfect spring tonic, when overwrought livers crave luxuriantly green food.

Daring souls may explore a startling option once prescribed by herbally-oriented doctors. "Urtication therapy" (stinging yourself with nettle *intentionally*) is similar to bee sting therapy. It awakens circulation, enlivens nerves and lymphatic flow, thereby easing congested, stiff areas (like arthritic joints). Any takers?

Really, for all the dread and fear, the occasional sting isn't that terrible. Pain can be relieved instantly using antidote plants grown nearby. (Chew briefly and apply the moist plant to the area.) For example, try "self heal"

(*Prunella vulgaris*), an attractive ground cover in the mint family. Those of scanty faith can keep Benadryl cream on hand.

If trying nettle sounds enticing to you, and you're tempted to overdo a good thing, don't. Overuse (more than two cups of tea a day) can dry you out. Keep in mind that no single remedy creates health—but in the meantime, inviting nettle into your life is an excellent beginning.

RESOURCES
WHERE TO GET NETTLE SEEDS:

Seeds of Change, P.O. Box 15700, Santa Fe, NM 87506-5700, toll free: 1-888-762-7333

Bountiful Gardens, 18001 Shafer Ranch Road, Willits, CA 95490-9626, (707) 459-6410

WHERE TO GET DRIED ORGANIC NETTLE LEAF:

Herbs, Etc., 1345 Cerrillos Rd., Santa Fe, NM 87505, 982-1265

The Herb Store, 107 Carlisle SE, Albuquerque, NM 87106, 255-8878

Many large health food stores also carry or can order nettle for you.

BEDTIME READING:

Healing Wise, by Susun Weed, Ash Tree Publishing, Woodstock, 1989. Includes 25 pages devoted to nettle, including uses for leaves, seeds and root, and recipes for cooked greens.

PART 3:

THE BEAUTIFUL
BALANCE OF BUGS

INTRODUCTION TO THIS SECTION:

I have uneasy feelings about a couple of these articles (written in 1995 and 1996). They perpetuate a sense of struggle against natural forces, and they contaminate the bugs themselves with human notions of "good" and "bad."

Consider this continuum of responses to bug "problems."

1. You kill the "bad" bugs with synthetic chemicals.
2. You kill or foil the "bad" bugs with natural stuff.
3. You get "good" bugs to do the killing for you.
4. You realize there's a balance between "good" and "bad" bugs, and you try to support that by inviting more "good" bugs into your yard.
5. You leave these dualities behind, focusing all your efforts on enhancing unstressed plant growth: improved soil quality, proper watering, companion planting, preventing heat/wind stress, etc.

As Eliot Coleman put it in the November/December 1998 issue of *Organic Gardening*: "Our current pest-control thinking is 180 degrees backwards. We should focus on the insusceptibility of plants rather than focus on killing pests. This approach can be defined as plant positive—in contrast to the present approach, which is pest negative...It's not a question of whether pesticides are undesirable or not. The fact is that they are superfluous."

Yes. And despite all our properly-focused efforts, we may still have problems as we head towards a more enlightened approach to our bug friends. Therefore, I offer you *all* the options for dealing with bug infestations.

• *NOTE: RESOURCES for this entire section appear on page 81*

WHY YOU SHOULD MANAGE, RATHER THAN WIPE OUT PESTS

Along with the warmer weather, it's safe to say that green shoots aren't the only things showing up in your garden. You can count on lots of bugs as well. Most people are aware that using insecticides carries some risk. But when aphids are covering that new rosebush, or hornworms are crawling all over your tomatoes, the impulse is strong and understandable to "do something." Fast.

But with gardens and the earth, "fast" doesn't always yield the best long-term results. A suggestion then: Don't panic. Take a minute to understand how bugs work in your garden, how your garden hosts the good and the bad, and how you may be able to play one off against another and, in the longer term, produce healthier, more productive plants.

Some background is helpful. Whenever we scratch the surface of an undisturbed natural system, a rich tapestry of interdependent relationships is revealed. Take Santa Fe 200 years ago: ample trees (piñon, juniper, etc.); diverse groundcovers and grasses; shrubs (Apache plume, saltbush, winterfat, mountain mahogany, and others); intact soil organisms; a great variety of insects, animals, birds, and reptiles. (The soils and vegetation of each region of New Mexico are different, of course, each shaped by its own geology, weather conditions and history.)

One key to longer term garden health is to imitate the diversity of the original ecosystem. Sadly, native vegetation is the frequent casualty of development or careless ranching. The earth is stripped, compacted, later eroded, and weeds form a scab on the disturbed soil. Insect and animal communities disappear, creating an imbalance between insects and their predators.

Enter the homeowner desiring a beautiful landscape and/or productive vegetable garden, asking "Why are these bugs ruining my plants?" The vast majority of infestations occur because something is wrong. Poor soil, improper plant placement, shallow watering, and absence of beneficial (predatory) insects are just a few possibilities.

Returning to our aphid-covered rosebush—ordinarily, the aphid's worst enemy should have taken care of the problem. (Have you hugged your ladybugs today?) Ladybugs eat not only aphids, but many other unwanted insects, leaving behind the beneficial ones. There are also lovely plants which attract ladybugs: buckthorn, euonymus, yarrow, butterfly weed, tansy, "Lemon Gem" marigolds and almost all herbs.

And there are other creatures that attract or encourage aphids. Ants, for example, tend and protect aphid colonies from predators while feeding on the honeydew the aphids produce. To control aphids, you must also discourage the ants. (*see* page 74)

But before you reach for the insecticide, consider too that "harmful" insects aren't all bad: Many actually draw beneficial insects to our gardens. Take hornworms, for instance. It works like this: A hornworm finds your tomato, then tiny parasitic wasps sniff out the worm, laying eggs in its body (or in the worm's eggs); this ends the hornworm's career. More than that, a few "bad" bugs stress the plants just enough to make them stronger. And leaf damage of up to 30% can actually increase the yield of some vegetable crops.

> **When we kill off the natural enemies of a pest, we inherit their work."**
>
> C. B. HUFFAKER

Which is why so many experts now prefer "managing" over wiping out pests. So don't automatically assume an unknown bug spells trouble. Only a little over 10% of all insects cause lasting damage.

So what's really wrong with spraying a synthetic insecticide on some of those bugs that're bugging you? First, it's no secret that ingesting chemical residues through air, food and water is harmful. This world really has no boundaries; poisons have a nasty habit of showing up in breast milk, wells, and other places. Some folks are deathly sensitive to chemicals. Further, if we poison insects, we also poison organisms living in the soil, birds, lizards and other partners in our ecosystem.

Just as important, even though chemicals *appear* to work, they usually make the original problem worse: Insecticides are agents of natural selection which weed out susceptible individuals, creating new generations of aggressive, invincible "superbugs." When chemicals kill both "bad" and "good" bugs, this eliminates the organisms that would help solve the original problem, and often results in a secondary outbreak of another unwanted insect.

If we work with nature, rather than succumbing to the impulse to control her manifestations which seem undesirable to us, the result will be much fewer problems in the long run.

GETTING BUGS TO
EAT EACH OTHER
INSTEAD OF YOUR PLANTS

Sucking, chewing, gnawing, drilling, nibbling ... It's alarming when bugs trash your treasured plants. But don't lose heart or pick up the insecticide. There's a better way to go: Invite (or purchase) "beneficial insects" to go to work for you. In the long run, nature's plan outperforms chemical sprays and doesn't kill all your friends—the good bugs, spiders, birds, toads and lizards. Here's how to get the bugs to eat each other instead of your plants.

It's astonishing, but more than half of all insects are predators or parasites of other insects. For appetizers, many of them enjoy nectar and pollen, same as bees and butterflies; for their main course, they dine on the bugs that are bugging you—aphids, grubs, cutworms and mites, to name a few. It's a good bet many of these great bugs are already hard at work in your yard.

Just like other living creatures, good bugs appreciate moisture, crave protection from wind and sun, and look for safe places to lay their eggs. By planting a multitude of shrubs, trees and perennials, as well as lots of small-blossomed herbs and wildflowers, you give these allies what they need—and may even persuade them to become permanent residents.

Many useful insects are minuscule; the old reliable petunias and snapdragons are too big for them to negotiate and contain relatively little pollen. Experiment instead with the parsley family (dill, Queen Anne's lace), the mints (thyme, peppermint, lemon balm), the sunflower family (yarrow, calendula, coreopsis, tansy, cosmos), and buckwheats (sulphur flower). Try to have at least one plant in flower from spring through fall.

Everyone's favorite garden helper is the ladybird beetle (ladybug). During the 20 days her larvae are maturing, they gobble up hundreds of aphids and have a taste for scales, whiteflies, thrips, leafhoppers and mites. Adults don't eat as much; they're too engrossed with mating and laying loads of eggs. Happily, adults can sometimes winter over in the garden.

But don't stop at ladybugs. Who'd suspect flies to be part of the cast of good guys? Tachinid flies, which resemble bristly houseflies, lay eggs which wind up inside unlucky hosts (tomato worms, many caterpillars, cutworms, even grasshoppers), and the hungry larvae feast on the victim from the inside out. The tiny Trichogramma wasp (it does *not* sting pets or people) has a ravenous appetite for upwards of 200 pests, including the cabbage worm, hornworm, corn earworm and borer, cutworm and codling moth. The wasp's larvae munch the eggs of unwanted pests, and your problem never materializes.

Some consider the delicately beautiful green lacewing, dubbed the "aphid lion," to be the best all-around predator. For up to 20 days, as the larvae mature, they devour aphids, red spider mites, thrips, immature scales and whiteflies, and the eggs of many worms. What about the entertaining praying mantis? Bad news. Turns out her appetite is small and undiscriminating—she eats beneficial bugs (and her mate) right along with a few beetles and tent caterpillars. Don't rely on her as your mainstay. And there's still more...Squash borers eating your  lunch? Bulbs and perennials gnawed by root maggots or grubs? Cutworms got you down? Beneficial nematodes (microscopic threadlike worms) can come to the rescue.

Insects aren't the only critters worthy of praise: Spiders and toads graze mostly on bad bugs, and lizards love ants. House wrens feed hundreds of caterpillars to their young. Bluebird moms offer grasshoppers to their fledglings, and adore cutworms and mosquitoes. Flickers snack on a thousand ants. And this is only a fraction of what happens behind the scenes in a healthy garden.

It's funny, but gardens *should* have bugs. All kinds. (Otherwise, the natural pest patrol won't stick around.) So relax and let the garden function naturally. Not that there's nothing to do: Handpick pests early to keep large numbers from overwhelming your predators. Learn to accept minor damage. Note successes and failures for next year. Practice waiting for the weather to change. Even bugs have their seasons—if ladybugs haven't polished off all the spring aphids, then the hot weather will. And remember, it's a bug-eat-bug world.

HOW TO OUTSMART YOUR BUGS
WITHOUT FOULING YOUR NEST

In the gardens of our dreams, weeds don't grow in flower beds (or driveways) and bugs don't bother our plants. When these things *do* happen, it's natural to want to get rid of the problem pronto, with one application of an inexpensive, foolproof product. The strongest products (like Diazinon and Sevin) do indeed make bugs drop dead, but not without exacting a heavy price from birds, bees, earthworms and other living things.

Fortunately, these days, a lot of gardeners are anxious to protect their health and the integrity of the environment. So it's no surprise there are numerous "safe" products and techniques, ranging from the ingenious to the macabre. Yes, they do take a little more involvement on your part—so give yourself credit for contributing to a healthier world. And consider that bugs can't develop resistance to many of these strategies—for instance, being trapped in sticky glue, or suffocated by an oily spray.

The cardinal rule is to catch whatever it is *early*, in order to avoid struggling with a full blown infestation.

To start, then, with a sure-fire tactic: Absolutely non-toxic and cost-free, hand-picking your bugs is underrated and extremely effective. Take a weekly stroll through the garden, closely inspecting one or two plants of each type, checking particularly under leaves, where eggs are often hidden. Early morning is an especially good time to find the cutworm culprit, always snoozing in the soil right next to the seedling it severed the night before...feed 'em to the birds.

I had trouble with asparagus beetles and found they were extremely easy to hand-pick. I held a container of soapy water underneath the asparagus frond and "tickled" the beetle until it dropped into the container.

A Good First Step

Don't forget to prevent pests from getting near vegetable and fruit crops in the first place; try netting, traps, row covers, cardboard collars for seedlings—even a strong jet of water (dislodges aphids). As well, try Tanglefoot, sticky stuff painted at the base of plants and trees to prevent invasion by larvae and to stop ants from introducing scales or aphids. Want to eat most of your pears, apples and peaches yourself? Get the ingenious sticky traps baited with pheromones (sexy smells insects use to attract mates) and lure destructive codling moths to their final resting place. Make a note to get your traps in early spring, before buds break.

Another strategy is disguising plants with unappealing tastes or odors. Apply some Hot Pepper Wax (an obvious effect), or better yet, spray with Seacrop, which repels insects *and* makes plants healthy. (You won't smell the seaweed, but the bugs will.) Remember, though, to wash off those plants before eating them.

Try growing plants that damaging bugs shun: herbs make wonderful, fragrant accents in the landscape; they draw beneficial insects, have few special needs, and are for the most part immune to infestations. Introduce garden sage, any of the thymes, lavender, tansy, rosemary (the "Arp" variety is perennial at this altitude), or the silvery *Artemisias* (wormwoods).

Still more options to discourage bugs: soapy sprays (like Safer's

Insecticidal Soap), Neem (keeps pupae and larvae from molting), diatoma-ceous earth (powdered silica that scratches and dehydrates bugs once they crawl through it), and lightweight horticultural oil (suffocates pests on orna-mentals, most vegetables and fruits). Unfortunately, these products also both-er or kill beneficial insects if they're on the plants being treated.

Best are those products which specifically target your chosen bug, yet are harmless to everything else. Grubs, various destructive worms and caterpil-lars are dispatched by the bacterium *Bacillus thuringiensis* (Bt). Another exam-ple is *Nosema locustae* ("Nolo Bait"), a naturally occurring spore that makes grasshoppers sick.

If you've tried everything and destructive insects continue to plague you, then bring out the bigger guns—plant-based insecticides like pyrethrum or rotenone. Though actually more deadly than the synthetic sprays (they kill good bugs and pond fish, and can harm *you*, so take care in applying), they're still much easier on the environment because they break down so quickly.

Even natural gardeners with the best pest management strategy—strong plants and healthy soil—occasionally need extra help. Since this year's bugs may be back again for dinner next year, at least with these tricks, you can make them think twice about it.

◆ ◆ ◆

Insects 101: GARDEN HEROES: THE LACEWING AND THE LADYBUG

Insects often get a bad rap. Their virtues (and amazing feats) are rarely dis-cussed. Most people assume an insect is guilty until proven innocent. But understanding insects better cultivates trust in nature's plan for pest con-trol and allows you to intervene where it really makes a difference. So in case you've hardened your heart against insects, here are intimate details of the fascinating (and endearing) interactions among several common garden inhabitants.

They're Insatiable

Everyone knows the ladybug (ladybird beetle), but few would recognize either her eggs or the larvae which hatch from them. Surprisingly, the larvae do much more good than the adults. The bright yellow eggs are oval and are laid standing on end in clusters of 10 to 20, in crevices of bark or underneath a leaf. Ladybugs often lay eggs on plants that aphids frequent—a wise move, since aphids are the larvae's favorite chow.

The young larvae have tapered, highly-segmented bodies less than a half-inch long, and sport tiny tufts of hairs and six legs. They are slate-colored, with red-orange markings. These lizard-shaped creatures are born starving and can put away up to 40 aphids per hour. If you find them wandering around looking for something to eat, transfer them to where they're needed.

After a few weeks of cleaning up your garden, they hang themselves up by their tails, form a protective case, and transform into an adult ladybug. Since the adult is no longer growing, it requires less food; however, it's still helpful in the garden.

Every year, ladybug larvae cause a lot of confusion. They're constantly brought into nurseries by alarmed gardeners who assume they're destructive, and want to know how to kill them.

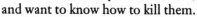

**ladybug and
her larva**

The ladybug is a rare exception in the world of creepy-crawlies—a well-loved insect. Its good reputation is upheld by the fact that it (and especially its larvae) eats aphids, and the eggs of many insects, including the Colorado potato beetle. And where are the good ladies when it turns cold? Having formed a layer of insulating fat under their wings, they take off to the mountains, where they hibernate in moist crevices in groups numbering in the thousands. (They retreat to the mountains in very hot, dry weather, as well.) When they awaken, their instincts compel them to fly until this layer of fat dissolves. This is why it's not too effective to buy those little bags of ladybugs at the nursery. You open the bag, and they all fly away. Furthermore, companies which sell them often harvest and deplete wild populations. It's better to wait for the ladybugs to find your garden, which they will, no matter where you live.

Even Hungrier

The golden-eyed lacewing has fragile, almost transparent wings, and a pale green body hardly more than a half-inch long. Its antennae point forward while large, brassy eyes stare to either side. The female lacewing lays her oval, greenish (later whitish) eggs in an unusual fashion—each stands upright on a long, thread-like stalk, resembling a miniature lollipop. The reason? If the eggs were clustered, the first voracious larva out would eat all the other eggs.

These characters resemble ladybug larvae in basic form but are all brown and have "giant" piercing jaws like miniature alligators. Aphid lions, as they are sometimes called, top ladybug larvae in aphid consumption (clocked by a highly motivated entomologist at 60 per hour), and they have a taste as well for mites, thrips, leafhoppers and assorted insect eggs. You won't get to watch this one, though: the aphid lion hides by day and feeds by night.

After almost two weeks of relentless feasting and a couple of molts, the larva makes a pearly, pea-sized cocoon. Two weeks later, the dainty, attractive lacewing emerges. Leaving its aggressive past behind, it flutters about looking for a mate, sips nectar and nibbles on pollen—a complete transformation. The lacewing (larva) is considered one of the best beneficial insects for the greenhouse or garden.

Ants Complete the Scenario

But let's get the whole story here. We can't talk about lacewings and ladybugs without talking about ants, because they compete for the same food source—aphids.

There are some varieties of ants which thrive on the aphid's honeydew (their sweet excretions after sucking plant sap). These ants are sometimes referred to as "pastoral." Like shepherds, they keep flocks of aphids, defend them from attack, and kill the aphids' parasites. Ants will even carry aphids from place to place, and protect aphid eggs in their nests over the winter, bringing them out again in the spring.

What do the ants get in return for their security services? When an ant gently strokes an aphid with its antennae, the aphid responds by excreting a drop of honeydew for the ant.

So if aphids are a problem in your garden, you probably have an ant problem as well. I once observed ladybugs approaching a cluster of aphids guarded by ants, and the ants knocked the ladybugs off the twig! Get out your magnifying glass and tune into the dramas in your yard instead of the ones on the Discovery Channel.

How to Give Beneficials the Edge

Here are some garden practices to help beneficial insects keep damaging insects in check. (Vegetable gardens may require further interventions that are beyond the scope of this article.)

• Mulch generously. Though mulch provides habitat for all insects, the "good" ones vastly outnumber the "bad" ones. However, if any plants had an insect problem, it's good garden hygiene to remove mulch and fallen leaves from underneath these plants at season's end. This prevents eggs or adults from over-wintering.

• Inspect the garden regularly. If you find unfamiliar insects or eggs, get them identified before doing anything. For instance, to take the proper action, you need to know whether the eggs you've found will become lady-bugs or Colorado potato beetles.

• Limit the use of pesticides to biological controls (such as Bt) which affect only the target pest. Remember, even plant-based pesticides like rotenone and pyrethrum kill good bugs.

• Don't disturb spiders or their webs. Spiders are unquestionably benefi-cial—all of them.

• Plan for a continuous supply of flowers in bloom. Ladybugs and lacewings (and many other insects like the highly beneficial, tiny parasitic wasps) require nectar and pollen. Three flowers good bugs like the best are Queen Anne's lace, yarrow and fennel; others include dill, cilantro, alyssum (one of the few early spring bloomers), coneflower, and anything in the mint family.

Cultivate Curiosity

Aside from ladybugs and lacewings, there are countless other friendly insects in the garden. Some I've yet to meet are robber flies, minute pirate bugs, soldier bugs, ambush bugs and assassin bugs. (Judging from their names, their lives must be dramatic.) While I'm not suggesting that all pest problems go away by themselves, there is a lot of help out there.

As I learn more about insects, fearful distrust has given way to curiosity and appreciation, and a hesitation to meddle unthinkingly with scenarios I don't fully understand.

◙ ◙ ◙

INTEGRATED PEST MANAGEMENT:
Cutting down on harmful pesticides

Though it's likely to be some time before safe methods of insect and weed control are the standard, a quiet revolution is occurring which is shifting the chemical-free-for-all model of pest management. Integrated Pest Management (IPM) is a key element in this change.

The Less Toxic the Better

While IPM doesn't exclude *sparing* use of synthetic pesticides, proper application of management principles makes that choice rarely necessary. IPM's greatest strength is in prevention: By promoting the health of the entire garden system, bugs stay in balance.

This is accomplished by a variety of common-sense practices such as generous mulching, proper watering, creating good soil as the foundation for plant health, planting flowers which draw natural predators, etc.

When problems do arise anyway, various methods are utilized, from the ridiculously simple (vacuuming bugs off of plants) to the sophisticated (pheromone traps). The least toxic options are tried first.

It helps to understand what causes problems which lead to more toxic options. Take the well-loved piñon tree. Critters for which natural controls are ineffective (like the Ips Beetle, or "borer") are often opportunistic, coming in for the final kill only after the tree is already weakened by improper care, injury, or outbreaks of other less deadly insects (like scale). When the piñon reaches the point of serious distress, it sends out chemical signals which tickle the receptors on bugs, even miles away. The borers are irresistibly drawn to the sick tree and go to work. These angels of mercy do not attack healthy plants. You just have to admire nature's carefully orchestrated plan for weeding out unhealthy players in the game.

Whenever bugs appear, IPM always counsels first correct identification, then monitoring, level-headed evaluation (deciding how much damage to plants is tolerable), and appropriate treatment if necessary. Remember, most bugs are not harmful, and few require action of any kind.

That is why Santa Fe entomologist Linda Wiener says, "I love to do nothing." For example, she feels tip moths on piñon trees are usually nothing to worry about. "Since the piñon has so many growing tips, the moths seldom reach high enough numbers to cause a problem. Besides, they have cycles. They may last a couple of years, then move on."

Don't let the apparent simplicity of this description fool you. Skilled IPM consultants are intimate with every minute detail of insect antics. They practice a highly refined art which insures effective results.

Canaries in the Mine

While many acknowledge the wisdom of the IPM approach, there's an unexpected factor which is hastening its adoption. The silent danger of pesticides is revealed increasingly by people who suffer most from their toxic effects, those with Multiple Chemical Sensitivity Disorder (MCS). Usually related to severe or cumulative exposure to chemicals, this chronic, serious condition includes extreme sensitivity to pesticides, a weakened immune and/or nervous system, and other disturbing symptoms.

Many consider people with MCS to be "canaries in the mine," giving the rest of us an urgent wake-up call as to how toxic our world has become. Disputes which arise over applying pesticides are often brought by MCS sufferers into the courts. And judges are increasingly ordering IPM policies instituted as part of the settlements, sometimes with surprisingly positive results.

They're Sold on IPM

Here's one inspiring story. For 40 years, a Santa Fe couple maintained extensive vegetable gardens, an orchard and landscape plants using a variety of pesticides, including Malathion. Several times a year, they courteously informed their neighbor when they would be "spraying" so he could close his windows. Things changed quickly a couple of years ago when the neighbor rented to someone with MCS. The final result was a court injunction forbidding the couple to use synthetic pesticides.

Instead, the court approved money for IPM consultant Mark Wood to aid the couple in making the transition to non-toxic pest control. Wood, who is manager of Payne's Nursery in Santa Fe, recalls the experience of working with these people. "The results were astounding. This couple was so excited by all they learned that they were totally sold on the new regime. Even after the injunction was finally lifted, they said they enjoyed this way of caring for their garden so much, they would never return to their former methods. They only wish the principles of IPM were more widely known."

Another incident involved a densely clustered community of 28 homes on five acres. There, someone wanted to spray a pesticide (Sevin) on a tree, and neighbors with MCS feared a relapse of their symptoms. The community responded by appointing a committee to come up with IPM guidelines as a basis for handling future bug problems. They also sponsored an IPM workshop and instituted a one year trial of the method.

Residents began crafting a policy which protects the community's health yet still leaves room for dialogue and conflict resolution. Despite the uncomfortable feelings elicited by this situation, the whole community learned a lot—and not just about bugs.

Shifting Paradigms

Many people still have a deep misunderstanding of bugs. Also, our culture's 50-year love affair with chemicals isn't going to end immediately. But there's some encouraging news out there. As a result of community pressure, the Santa Fe Public School System is abandoning routine pesticide applications and switching to IPM. The University of New Mexico has been on board with IPM for its buildings and grounds for a year and a half with excellent results. More and more nurseries are training their employees and educating their customers.

Let's hope these trends continue and we can kick the pesticide habit soon.

RESOURCES

Many of our nurseries are gold mines of information. Ask to talk to the person most knowledgeable about native plant communities and natural pest control.

Common Sense Pest Control: Least toxic solutions for your home, garden, pets and community, by William Olkowski, et al, Taunton Press, Newtown, 1991. Considered by bug experts to be one of the best books.

ecoGarden: Safe alternatives to pesticides and more, by Nigel Dudley and Sue Stickland, Avon Books, 1991. $10.00

Rodale's Color Handbook of Garden Insects, by Anna Carr, Rodale Press, Emmaus, PA, 1979. $14.95. Excellent color photos of insects, from eggs to adults, with a key for easy identification.

Northwest Coalition for Alternatives to Pesticides, P.O. Box 1393, Eugene, OR 97440 (541) 344-5044. An outstanding educational resource.

Organic Gardening Magazine, (800) 666-2206. A good source of chemical-free suggestions.

ENTOMOLOGISTS provide the most reliable bug identification. Here are northern New Mexico's best:

The Bug Lady (Linda Wiener), e-mail: thebuglady@aol.com, 984-2371. Besides insect identification, she advises on non-toxic pest control, teaches classes, and offers short phone consultations.

Call the State Forestry Department, 476-3332, and ask to talk to their entomologist.

In the Albuquerque area, entomologist **Dick Fagerlund** can help you. Call him at UNM, 277-9904, or e-mail, fagerlun@unm.edu

BENEFICIAL INSECT SUPPLIERS (buy your bugs at the FIRST sign of infestation):

The Cooperative Extension Service can help you locate suppliers for direct purchase of beneficial insects. Albuquerque, 275-2576; Santa Fe, 471-4711

The Green Spot, 93 Priest Rd., Nottingham, NH 03290-6204, 603-942-8925. *The Green Methods Manual*, (online at *www.greenmethods. com*) is the bug primer par excellence, and contains the most detailed information for the layman I've ever seen. To order bugs and products: *www.shopgreenmethods.com*.

Peaceful Valley Farm Supply, P.O. Box 2209, Grass Valley, CA 95945, (888) 784-1722

Planet Natural, P.O. Box 3146, Bozeman, MT 59772 (800) 289-6656. Experts in natural pest control.

Gardens Alive! (812) 537-8650. Very informative catalogue.

HOW TO MAKE YOUR OWN BUG SPRAYS

Food for beneficial insects: If you don't have enough nectar-producing plants yet, try this simple approach to attract ladybugs and lacewings: Dissolve a half-cup sugar in one quart water. Apply with a watering can to plants where aphids are a problem.

Bug sprays: Rather than buy sprays, it's easy to make your own. The variations are endless, but there are several basic types: soap sprays, oil sprays which suffocate insects, and stinky or distasteful sprays which cause insects to avoid the plants.

Plain soap spray: Any dishsoap in a one to two percent solution can be used for aphids, whitefly, mites, scales, pear slugs, leafhoppers, harlequin bugs, squash bugs, etc. (Some sources recommend washing soapy sprays off the plants after 10 minutes to avoid burning leaves.)

Basic stinky spray: In a quart jar, place several smashed garlic cloves, a diced onion, a diced Jalapeño pepper (or one Tablespoon cayenne pepper). Fill jar with water and let sit until it begins to ferment. Strain mixture. Before spraying on plants, add one teaspoon liquid detergent.

Basic oil spray: In a glass jar, mix together one cup vegetable oil (anything except olive or sesame) and one Tablespoon of dishsoap. This is your stock solution. Shake well, add one to two teaspoons to one cup water. (Caution: may damage waxy plants.)

Even though these sprays are non-toxic to the environment, they will hurt or kill beneficial insects. Some could damage leaves if sprayed on a hot, sunny day. It's better to spray in the cool of morning or evening.

PART 4:

WATER CONSERVATION STRATEGIES

GETTING A GRIP ON DRIP IRRIGATION

Originally developed to raise food in extremely arid climates, drip-irrigation systems are increasingly popular in both landscape and vegetable gardens. What's so good about them? A carefully managed system results in thriving plants and stunted water bills. Here's how to get started with this valuable technology.

How It Works

As you might imagine, the system delivers water drip by drip, slowly enough for the earth to absorb all of it. The effect is like a gentle rain that penetrates deeply, but only at the root zones of your plants. (Conventional sprinklers deliver water at around 10 times the rate of a drip-irrigation system, wetting everything in sight.)

There are many advantages: no loss of sprayed water to wind; ideal for slopes; and (when plants are well-mulched) almost zero evaporation. Further, unless you own a fully landscaped "estate," these do-it-yourself drip systems are relatively inexpensive (under $100). They require minimal maintenance, are adaptable (for those who endlessly tinker with a garden's evolution), and can even be automated when you're traveling.

Common Drip Bummers: How to Avoid Them

Clogging of emitters is probably the most common problem. The reasons for this can vary. "Laser tubing" has an inherent tendency to clog and should be avoided. ("Bi-wall" has the same bad habits.) Water with high sediment or mineral levels can leave a deposit: remove affected emitters and soak in a 2:1 solution of vinegar to water. Burying emitters not specially designed for underground use can lead to problems, too.

Sometimes, instead of clogging, there will be leaks, floods and geysers. Depending on how long a leak remains undiscovered, hundreds (or thousands) of gallons of water can be wasted. Causes for these mishaps can be traced to gnawing dogs, rabbits with the gene for "chewing black tubes when thirsty," lines which are trampled and separated from their connectors, or even overzealous gardeners wielding a sharp shovel. To avoid unnecessary loss of water, occasionally stroll around your garden while the system is running, to make sure everything's okay.

Nuts and Bolts

For a drip novice, a visit to Sisco or The Firebird (retail drip-irrigation stores) can be daunting. First, there's all those little boxes full of tiny plastic gizmos labeled with cryptic terms. Then, it becomes apparent that some higher math will be involved (fractions, multiplication, changing liters to gallons, etc.). Hang in there—you won't need a degree in hydraulics. It's really as simple as Legos, unless you get fancy with variations like bubblers, sprayers, and "ooze tubing."

Do drop by these stores—you'll get superior components, expert advice, and knowledgeable trouble-shooting. Both shops consider Hardie or Rainbird to be excellent brands. Don't pinch pennies and dimes when buying components; you'll pay for it later in dollars and headaches.

Keep it Simple

It's possible to concoct multizoned irrigation schemes which vary in duration and frequency for each type of landscape element. These plans require miles of tubing and a computerized timer more sensitive than a moody lover. I'd advise sacrificing this type of precision for simplicity of operation.

For example, I use several hundred feet of 1/2-inch tubing that snakes all around the house to various garden areas. It's above ground, but invisible

---

SOME LIMITS TO CONSIDER
1/2" tubing: maximum run-500 feet
For 500 feet of 1/2" tubing: maximum gph-300
3/16" line: maximum run-25 feet
Tubing with in-line emitters: maximum run-33 feet
1/8" line: maximum run - 10 feet
Minimum PSI for emitters to work: 5 PSI (some say 7 or 8 PSI)
For every 100' of 1/2" line, you lose 3-4 pounds pressure.

under mulch, and easily accessed when I need to make adjustments. For years, the whole system was turned on at once from my hose bib. When the line became too long for one pressure regulator (*see* box on Limits), I split it into two zones, each with its pressure regulator and filter. Still simple.

Each plant receives water from 1/2, 1 or 2-gallon-per-hour (gph) emitters. Larger trees need two or three 2 gph emitters. Since my soil is surprisingly sandy, (*see* Fine Tuning), I run the system three times a week for about an hour and twenty minutes, depending on the weather. I've successfully established all kinds of plants on this schedule.

Lawns require a different approach. Check with a drip specialist (or better yet, grow a lawn which doesn't require water). Further, brand-new plantings need supplemental hand-watering between scheduled irrigation days for the first two weeks.

Drip Irrigation for Vegetable Gardens

What's wrong with the old-fashioned hose? For one thing, watering from overhead compacts the soil. Then there's the loss to evaporation. Further, drip irrigation reduces problems with "salty" mineral deposits on top of the soil. Try it and see if your vegetables don't respond dramatically. Mine did.

Most vegetables are annuals and lack extensive root systems; and many have large, succulent leaves. For these reasons, they are not drought-tolerant, and they need a more frequent irrigation schedule than perennials. During hot weather, irrigate two or three times a day, but for short periods. The smallest amount of water delivered by an emitter is 1/2 gallon per hour—an amount which could easily overwhelm a tender seedling. Fifteen minutes (delivering two cups of water at each emitter) would probably be the maximum time you'd want to run this system at one time.

Fine Tuning

We know what happens when plants get too little water. But what about too much? Mary Butler, co-owner of The Firebird, cautions, "You don't want to be able to wring water out of the soil—this ruins the air spaces in it, and isn't good for the plants." Check things out with a trowel to avoid over watering. Ultimately, you can kill a plant with what seems like kindness.

To complicate things, water behaves differently in different soils. Ask the nursery how much water to apply, then fine-tune to your soil's needs. Always let the top one to three inches of soil dry out between waterings.

Coarse, sandy soil has a loose structure, and gravity pulls the water straight down. This type of soil drains and dries out fast. You will need to irrigate for shorter time periods, more often. The goal is to get water down to the root zone, but not past it.

Clay soil absorbs water very slowly, so moisture spreads laterally before penetrating deeply. This type of soil stays wet longer. You must run the system longer and less often.

(Do water heavily occasionally to drive salts down below the root zone.)

Smart Gardening

Our native plants have strategies for conserving water—let them conserve it. Surprisingly, these plants become stronger when brought to the point of wilting before watering... just don't go too far.

The lion's share of residential water goes onto summer gardens. Drip-irrigation systems can help reduce this amount. Another place we can make a difference is at the nursery, where a plant's water needs can affect our decisions. Just because a plant is for sale doesn't mean it's appropriate to plant it this summer. Indeed, in arid lands, the best use of a drip system is to help establish drought-resistant plants for a year or two, and then let the plants do what they do best.

One caution about this time-saving, wonderful invention: As is common with technologies that do things for us, the result is less involvement with the subject (your plants) than before. You won't notice if an emitter clogged until your plant expires. Even worse, if a big line comes apart, or a small line pops off (which seems to happen most often in early spring when water in lines may freeze occasionally), you'll lose MEGA amounts of water—hundreds of gallons per hour—defeating a major reason you switched to drip in the first place, to save water. So please take that stroll often to make sure everything's working okay.

What to Buy

• Filter: Prevents sediment from entering the line. The dealer will advise on cleaning. A "Y-filter" with a flushing mechanism is the best. ($12-$25)

• Pressure regulator: Takes household pressure down to a manageable 30 pounds per square inch (PSI). Without it, you'll blow connections in your system, resulting in the floods mentioned in this article. For the short lines required in vegetable gardens, a 15 PSI regulator is fine. ($8-$10)

• 1/2-inch "poly" tubing: Strong yet flexible; carries water to planted areas. There you'll tap into the line with an emitter, or attach smaller tubing (1/4-inch or 3/16-inch) to go a few feet in one direction or another. "Elbow" and "tee" connections allow branching and turns in the line. Finally, at the end of the 1/2-inch line, a fitting closes it. (One-half-inch line costs 14 cents a foot; other components cost pennies.)

• "Drip-in" line: Useful for rows or beds of vegetables. Contains built-in emitters spaced 6 or 12-inches apart. Never clogs.

• Emitters: Calibrated to deliver variable amounts of water, from 1/2 to two gallons per hour (gph). Three basic styles, under 50 cents each:

"*Turbulent flow*" are partially pressure-compensating; these perform well.

"*Diaphragm*" are pressure-compensating, necessary if your land has more than a 12-foot elevation change.

"*Vortex*" clog easily; avoid these.

• Pinch clamps for 1/2-inch line: Prevents big lines from wiggling loose from their connections—a must when the lines are exposed to the elements. (20 cents each) (A low cost alternative is to twist baling wire around the connections.)

• Pinch clamp pliers: To attach clamps to line. ($6.25)

RESOURCES
Sisco, 4610 McLeod NE, Albuquerque, 881-4050

The Firebird, 1808 Espinacitas, Santa Fe, 983-5264

Free publication: "***Drip Irrigation — THE BASICS***" by Tom Bressan, available at The Firebird (This 1988 publication does not contain information on the newest drip technology, but is still extremely clear and useful for a basic understanding.)

Reprints from ***Sunset Magazine***, 80 Willow Road, Menlo Park, CA 94025, (415) 321-3600. "***Straight Talk About Drip***," July '92; "***Drought Survival Guide for Home and Garden***," 1991.

STORING RAINFALL
ABOVE THE GROUND

In June, when a relatively wet spring is nothing but a damp memory, I'll still have rainwater coming out the end of my hose. By installing a series of tanks under my canales, I've saved amazing amounts of the water plants love best.

Beyond the 33-Gallon Trash Can
When I got serious about water conservation, I first considered a buried cistern. The steep price and potential disturbance of my land by large machinery prompted me to reconsider the old-fashioned rain barrel. (Of course, in many situations, an underground cistern is a viable option.) I chose stock tanks for my project.

Galvanized metal stock tanks (20 gauge, two feet tall, in oblong or round shapes) offer the most flexibility in design, are relatively attractive when painted to match the house stucco, and cost between 40 and 70 cents per gallon of storage capacity. Tanks range from 70 to over 400 gallons, vastly outperforming the 33 gallon trash can.

To design your system, first figure out how much water you can collect. One thousand square feet of roof surface yields 625 gallons of water per inch rainfall. Don't worry about having enough storage to hold a year's worth of rain, because you'll use up the water in between rains. (My roof generates almost 10,000 gallons per year, but my storage capacity is only 1,300 gallons.)

In a downpour, small tanks fill almost immediately, so backup storage is smart. After my smaller tanks are full, the water is transferred into a 400 gallon (covered) round tank which I've tucked in among some trees.

Snow melt can fill up your tanks, too. (Ten to twelve inches of snow translates to one inch of rain.) Whereas trash cans full of water swell and split when they freeze, stock tanks won't. However, before winter, remove any galvanized fittings and faucets—these *will* burst.

During the coldest months, my tanks have a thick layer of ice on top. Whenever winter temperatures rise enough, the ice melts so I can get a pump into the tank to water my trees. By March, I usually still have 400 gallons of water (snow melt) ready to use as my plants come back to life.

So how does water get from the tanks to the garden? Though I occasionally use a watering can to tend to an individual plant, I like the ease of a submersible utility pump with a hose attached to it. Keep in mind that as you go uphill and/or further from the pump, fewer gallons per minute will flow from the hose.

In choosing a pump, consider the pressure (PSI rating), the gallons per minute it delivers, and how far uphill it can pump. Talk to someone who can help you sort out the dizzying diversity of pumps available.

A slow-flow option for distributing the water is to use gravity feed, possible only if tanks are uphill from your garden. In this case, the threaded openings near the bottom of the stock tanks

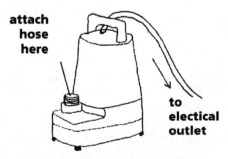

attach hose here

to electical outlet

One type of submersible utility pump

accommodate galvanized nipples, and an adapter converts pipe threads to hose threads. Attach a faucet, then your hose.

Setting the Tanks

To prepare the tanks, clean them inside and out with a soft cloth dampened with plain vinegar, to remove the layer of protective oil. Then, if desired, paint only the outside with a product made for galvanized metal.

Water is heavy; make sure the bottom of each tank is firmly supported, and not resting on any sharp rocks. Do *not* set tanks on ashes, cinders or cinder blocks—the galvanized metal will corrode. I set my tanks on a level bed of sand and very fine gravel ("crusher fines").

Providing shade for tanks does slow down evaporation and algae buildup, but shade is not absolutely necessary. Tall, ornamental grasses are one good choice. Screen the tanks so water gets in, but leaves, bugs, lizards and squirrels stay out. I use 1/8" hardware cloth with shade cloth stretched over it (to prevent algae growth). Even though it spatters a bit, the lion's share of the water still goes into the tanks. Please take extra precautions if children will be near the tanks.

Not All Water is Created Equal

Why do plants respond dramatically to rainwater, even if they're getting their proper ration of ground water? Well water in this area is alkaline and full of "dissolved solids" (minerals like iron sulfite, sodium chloride, potassium sulfate). Our already alkaline soil has no need for yet more minerals, which build up in the soil over time. Rainwater, on the other hand, has almost no dissolved solids, is slightly acidic and full of oxygen (and contains a form of nitrogen). But a mineral-burdened soil couldn't explain why plants perk up after even a light rain. Perhaps how rain is formed provides a clue. As trees and plants transpire (exhale) water through their life processes, tiny bits of organic matter such as leaf dust, pollen and bacteria are released. These particles provide the nuclei around which raindrops form.

Though my botany book tells me that little water is absorbed by most leaves, I suspect leaves receive certain subtle elements through their pores from rain.

So, back to the rain in your storage tanks—Here's a commonly asked question: Is it safe to irrigate vegetables with water off a tarred roof? Santa Fe Engineer George Naugles, familiar with most aspects of water treatment and re-use, knows of no research on this question. However, he comments, "I wouldn't hesitate to eat vegetables I grew with water off my tarred roof. A soil rich in organic matter excels at absorbing any contaminants in roof water."

But since water can sit on a flat roof and gather bacteria, I avoid spraying roof water directly on salad greens I'm about to eat. And for heaven's sake, don't drink the stuff!

RESOURCES
STOCK TANKS:
  Santa Fe: **Feed Bin** 982-0511
  Albuquerque: **Town & Country Feed Store** 296-6711

PAINT:
  Diamond-Vogel makes a superior water-based product and matches it to your stucco color for $20 per gallon. Only one coat of this combination primer/topcoat is necessary. Apply after wiping outside of tank with vinegar-dampened cloth. In Santa Fe: 781 W. San Mateo, 983-8113. In Albuquerque: 1016 3rd St. NW, 243-1000

SYSTEM DESIGN & INSTALLATION:
  In Santa Fe: ·**Daniel Owsiany, 438-3488**
        The Firebird, 1808 Espinacitas, 983-5264
  In Albuquerque: **Tony C de Baca,** 281-4341; **TP Pumps,** 1824 2nd St. NW, 247-4036.

NOTE: You can use stored rainwater for drip irrigation systems, but you'll need a special filter, along with a pump which won't burn out under the restricted flow of these systems. Talk to TP Pumps or The Firebird.

❖ ❖ ❖

STORING RAINFALL IN THE GROUND WITH PUMICE WICKS

Every summer, an unbelievable amount of water hurtles off the roof. It rushes out of reach into storm drains or arroyos, sometimes leaving a wide path of erosion in its wake. A week or two later, after things have dried out, there you stand, drawing water through the hose at five gallons (or more) per minute, out of an overtaxed aquifer. Foolish, isn't it?

This tremendous rainfall resource can be slowed, captured and even stored, using a variety of low tech, inexpensive alternatives. The first line of defense, the French drain, is essentially a gravel-filled unlined trench or hole. The drain is traditionally placed under canales or next to driveways or other surfaces which shed a lot of water. Though it prevents erosion and improves the availability of water in soil immediately surrounding it, the French drain's storage capacity is limited.

Create an Underground Sponge

More often than not, the water comes off the canale in one spot today, and you need it two weeks later, 10 or 15 feet away. Surprisingly, one of the most efficient and convenient places to store water is in the ground itself. One way to do it is with an adaptable, expanded version of the French drain. A gravel-filled, buried bucket collects water from the canale and guides it through a PVC pipe into one or more narrow, long trenches filled with pumice (a porous, lightweight volcanic rock). The pumice is covered by a thick layer of newspaper, then soil. As water flows into the trench, it spreads by gravity and capillary (wicking) action—hence, this invention is dubbed a "pumice wick."

Pumice, with its abundant air spaces, absorbs and stores water like an underground sponge, where it can't evaporate. As the surrounding soil dries out, water is released gradually—sometimes over a period of up to six weeks—to trees and shrubs planted around the perimeter of the narrow "wicks." Ground covers can be planted in the shallow layer of soil on top of the trenches. (Pumice wicks won't work for lawns, which need an evenly distributed supply of water over a broad area.)

As a side note, ecologically savvy gardeners may take issue with using pumice. Found in deposits in and around the Jemez Mountains, it has been pit-mined, after all, sometimes with detrimental consequences to the land. However, deposits are usually less than 20 feet deep, and regulations now require the land to be reshaped, reclaimed and reseeded after pumice is removed. Check into the condition of your local supply site.

Runaway Landscaping

Nate Downey founded Santa Fe Permaculture in 1992 and has been installing various systems to capture rainwater ever since. Heavy rainfall one July created some crisis situations for him to handle. "Because driveways generate such a tremendous amount of runoff, when they're uphill from the house, erosion damage is very common. After a big rain, I get frantic calls from people whose new landscaping slid onto their patio." Other people call him for help when their land and gardens slide not towards, but away from the house.

"It's a big problem," says Downey, "when people decide to live on top of a mountain. The contractor usually slices off the top of the site and spreads out the extra dirt. The house itself may be on solid soil, but the water coming off that house—with some force—invariably hits loose fill dirt and begins to expose the foundation." Actually, all new construction, mountains or not, ends up with "trashy, loose soil" around it, which can lead to some serious erosion problems. The remedy for runaway landscaping is to direct water into the ground as soon as possible, and allow plants to use it.

The Case for Integrated Design
Sadly, the design of a home often bears little relationship to the forces of the surrounding environment—sun, rain, wind—or to the needs and interests of its occupants. On the other hand, a fully integrated design can lead to joys and comforts far beyond simply stopping erosion and growing some nice bushes ten feet from your canale. Good design has to do with recognizing resources, problems and needs, and then making the connections among them.

Here are some examples of how a French drain/pumice wick could transform a "problem" (that is the problem of "too much" rainwater) into a benefit for you and your home.

• Support deciduous trees to shade and cool south or west sides of the house.

• Train insulating evergreen vines such as winter creeper (*Euonymus fortunei*) onto walls which are hot in summer, cold in winter.

• Plant fruit trees on the north side of the house, where they'll come out of dormancy later in the spring and avoid frost damage.

• Plant berries like currant or chokeberry, then watch the show of wild birds as they feed near the house.

• Protect your home with a rainwater-fed firebreak.

...The possibilities are endless.

Remember, every 1,000 square feet of impermeable surface sheds 625 gallons of water per inch of rainfall. Measure your roof (and your driveway, too), then go ahead—indulge in some great fantasies of what you will grow with all that free water.

How to Create a French Drain/Pumice Wick
Please note that this technology is only about five years old...these directions and dimensions can be changed to suit your particular circumstances. However, do take care to maintain all proportions and relationships as shown in the illustrations.

Buy a lightweight galvanized metal bucket or bin which holds 15-20 gallons—about 18" deep, 24" wide. (Plastic containers can also work.) Remove handle(s). Use heavy snips to cut hole(s) just under 4" diameter, where you want the wick(s) to extend, and so that the hole ends up near the top of the trench holding the pumice. (*see* Figure 1)

Under the canale, dig a hole to hold the bucket. Dig trench(es) for the pumice. Trenches are a shovel's width wide (8-10") and around 16-18" deep,

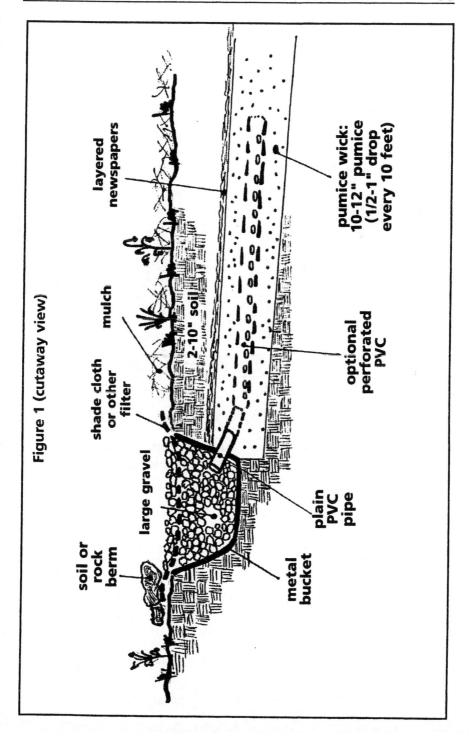

Figure 1 (cutaway view)

layered newspapers

mulch

shade cloth or other filter

2-10" soil

large gravel

soil or rock berm

metal bucket

plain PVC pipe

optional perforated PVC

pumice wick: 10-12" pumice (1/2-1" drop every 10 feet)

and can be dug in straight or curved lines. They should drop 1/2 to 1" every 10 feet. This helps accommodate heavy summer storms which drop lots of rain, fast. Keep the trenches at least 2 1/2 to 3 feet away from the house. (The greater the area of roof drained by each canale, the more trenches filled with pumice are needed to radiate off each French drain, to accommodate the water.) (*see* Figure 2)

Trenches longer than 20 feet should have perforated PVC pipes running down the middle of the pumice so water will be released evenly along the length of the wick. If you want to use water far from the canale, the location

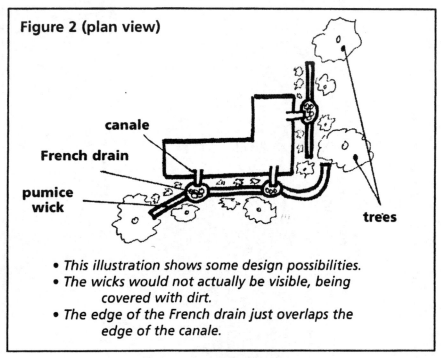

Figure 2 (plan view)

canale

French drain

pumice wick

trees

- *This illustration shows some design possibilities.*
- *The wicks would not actually be visible, being covered with dirt.*
- *The edge of the French drain just overlaps the edge of the canale.*

must be downhill. Run 4" (unperforated) pipe from the canale to drain to the area, then begin the pumice wick.

Now add 10 - 12" pumice to the bottom of the trench. Layer newspaper *over* the pumice, overlapping it well—it should be about 20-24 sheets thick. This prevents dirt from clogging the pumice. It's unnecessary to line the bottom or sides with newspaper. Finally, backfill the trench with dirt (over the newspaper) and tamp it down gently.

An important finishing touch is to add an extra rim of gravel and/or a large rock berm around the outside of the gravel-filled bucket. This further protects the French drain from silting in with soil.

The costs? Pumice wicks run up to $10 per foot, installed, and the French drains are $125 each, installed. (This doesn't include the optional rock berm.)

RESOURCES

If you don't want to do the work yourself, these folks can help: In Albuquerque, **Jim Brooks**, 281-8425; in Santa Fe, **Nate Downey**, 424-4444

For other applications of French drains and pumice wicks, see *Permaculture Drylands Journal*, Issue #16, Winter '91-'92, "Water Harvesting for Dryland Cities." Send $6.00 to PDJ, P.O. Box 156, Santa Fe, NM 87504-0156.

◈ ◈ ◈

Making The Most of Your Water:
GARDENING WITH DROUGHT

When rainfall is particularly sparse, gardeners and their gardens suffer from drought-induced anxiety. But if you plant intelligently, you can cut down on water use significantly and keep (most of) your garden from expiring.

Appropriate Scale and Choices

There is a human need for lush areas (the Garden of Eden?), especially in arid climates. Here in New Mexico, we can limit these areas to an appropriate scale. In some desert countries these needs are met with an enclosed, densely-planted courtyard, shaded overhead by trees or lattice. It's worth noting that in these places, gathering rainwater is commonplace. (I'd love to see more New Mexican communities which rely heavily on non-renewable groundwater resources consider this sensible practice.) Water can be stored in a variety of ways, above, below or in the ground. Using grey water is another option, albeit with certain restrictions and cautions. Many books are available on this topic.

A small, well-designed, protected garden space retains moisture and is easily maintained with scarce resources. So place thirstier plants in your little Garden of Eden.

For the broad landscape, use drought-tolerant plants native to the part of New Mexico you live in, and include water catchments for them, such as swales and berms. Be aware that nurseries sell plants with a whole range of water needs. They are often caught between customers' unrealistic desires (fanned by magazines featuring gardens in water-rich areas) and the store's philosophy to convert people to appropriate plant choices.

We have countless lovely water misers to choose from. Just a few of the least thirsty are sand sage, winter fat, desert beard tongue, desert four o'clock, blackfoot daisy, chocolate flower, sand verbena, beargrass, blue grama grass, and of course, the cacti.

Strategies

First and foremost, soils must be created which can drink deeply of available water and retain it, like a sponge. Briefly, this means adding lots of organic matter and a thick mulch.

To make the most of the water you do apply, cluster plants together as much as possible. Not only do they look better, but they'll also shade and protect each other from desiccating winds. Cover any bare dirt pathways to prevent the water you use from being "wicked" into adjoining dry areas. Shredded tree bark makes a nice, soft path, and is inexpensive (or free) from companies which trim trees. Gravel is also an option; I find tan gravel the most attractive. Consider making garden beds lower than surrounding pathways so they retain moisture.

In terms of efficient delivery systems, drip irrigation and soaker hoses (especially when placed under a mulch) are far superior to overhead sprinklers. (Taking drip irrigation one step further, some emitters can even be buried in the soil—I'd bury the line only an inch or two.) A large percentage of finely sprayed water simply evaporates instantly—especially when humidity hovers at less than 10%, as it often does in New Mexico. It's ideal to irrigate deeply and infrequently. Rather than 10 to 30 minutes a day, every day, as some advise, it's far better to run the system two to three times a week for a longer period of time—clay soils less often, sandy soils more often. (see page 86) This encourages the formation of deep root systems—literally life insurance for your plants.

Be brave—go ahead and wean established drought-tolerant plants off of all irrigation, but don't force them to go cold turkey. Instead, water them the same volume, less and less frequently. I'm experimenting with the minimum thresholds for various shrubs, vines and trees.

One important tool is a moisture meter. Available from nurseries, a meter can tell you exactly what's happening five or six inches underground. Even when the surface of the ground is dry to the touch, there may be enough moisture at root level. Result: You water only when it's needed.

Because plants have differing needs, it's important to provide a variety of garden microclimates, using half-walls, hedges, fences, large rocks, sunken areas, etc. One strategy for establishing small, individual plants is to form a "rock mulch" by surrounding the stem with several rocks which are at least three inches across (don't allow rocks to touch the stem). On cool nights, there will be some condensation, affording the plant a little extra moisture. The rocks keep the ground cool and damp, prevent evaporation, and protect soil organisms. Roots will proliferate happily under the rocks.

The most important microclimate to create is at the soil level with the use of mulch. Choose whatever type you prefer—compost, straw, shredded bark—just make sure it's at least two to three inches thick so it will conserve soil moisture. A straw mulch is probably the coolest, as it reflects light.

Drought in the Vegetable Garden

There are many innovative techniques to save precious water and keep crops from expiring. Consider trying some of these ideas, invent your own, and let me know of your successes.

• Bury a one gallon *unglazed* earthenware pot (plug the drainage hole) so that the top is level with the soil surface. Fill it with water, put a saucer on top, and plant seedlings one and a half inches from its edge. Moisture seeps out slowly into the soil; the pot is refilled as needed.

• For fruit trees, create narrow holes 12 inches deep and three inches wide, at three points at the drip line (underneath the outermost branches). Fill holes with gravel and/or sand, mark the spots and mulch well. Slowly soaking these spots takes water straight to the root zone.

• One gardener I know slows evaporation by placing weed barrier cloth over her drip lines. She cuts holes in the cloth and plants squash seedlings or potatoes in the soil below.

• Recessed planting beds have long been used by indigenous cultures in arid lands; give them a try.

• Dappled shade from trees such as locust or New Mexico privet protects plants from harsh sun. Other options are shade cloth (40 to 60% density) or "row covers" which afford shelter from both sun and wind.

• Windbreaks are a necessity. A semi-permeable hedge works best.

• Plant corn in a deep hole (eight to 12 inches deep); as it grows, gradually fill the hole to cover the stem but not the leaves. Roots will develop along the stalk, helping the corn to resist drought. Hopi corn works especially well for this type of planting.

• Plant tomato seedlings so only the top few leaves are above ground. Extensive roots will develop along the deeply buried stem.

• Choose appropriate crops that tolerate conditions in the southwest. Swap seeds with local gardeners. We can develop our own locally-adapted strains. Grow amaranth for greens and grain: during intense heat, amaranth closes its leaf pores to conserve water. Focus on heat-tolerant crops such as New Zealand spinach, sunflower, orach, etc.

Cultivating Flexibility

Extreme weather calls for conserving scarce resources, and that includes yours, too. What can you afford to give during a heat wave? Have poor plant choices or watering techniques made you a slave to your garden? Do you hide the water bill from your mate? If so, it's time to explore what it really means to live within the limits of this landscape. (For example, during the 1996 drought, I reluctantly set aside plans for a vegetable garden in lieu of constructing better shelter from wind and sun for the next year's garden.) Cultivate some flexibility about what you think your garden should look like. Exercise your critical eye. Observe what's doing well, analyze why, and repeat those techniques (or plants) in other areas.

And now for the sad part. After mulching your plants to the gills and cutting down on water use for a few weeks, it will be time to evaluate. Observe what's ailing, and let it go. Yes, I mean die. California's drought lasted seven years. If they could let their lawns die, we can let our less hardy plants go, too. Take heart—we'll all be risking (and losing) our plants together, as we allow space to be opened for the truly tough plants.

RESOURCES
DROUGHT-TOLERANT PLANTS:

All of our local nurseries carry drought-tolerant plants, but a few places take it one step further by collecting local seeds and growing the plants in their greenhouses or on their farms. These plants tend to outperform those brought in from other areas. Be sure to visit the Xeriscape Demonstration Garden at Santa Fe Greenhouses!

DO-IT-YOURSELF DRIP IRRIGATION SPECIALISTS:
Santa Fe: **The Firebird**, 1808 Espinacitas, 983-5264
Albuquerque: **Sisco**, 4610 McLeod NE, 881-4050

BOOKS:
The Enchanted Xeriscape, free booklet on water-wise plants, (800)-WATER-NM.
How-To Guide to Xeriscaping, a free, 48-page booklet published by the Water Conservation Office in Albuquerque, 768-3655.
Gardening the Arid Land, by Robert Gerard, Brooker Publishing, La Mesa, 1997. This highly practical book is a must for vegetable gardeners.

PART 5:

RELATING TO THE COMMUNITY & THE EARTH

SOME THOUGHTS ON RECLAIMING LAND ON A BROAD SCALE

R estoring a neglected vegetable garden or repairing construction damage provides a tangible measure of satisfaction. But some folks are captivated by the idea of healing much larger chunks of the landscape. Land restoration has become a big issue in the southwest. To accomplish it simply and without causing more problems, we must make room for a new understanding of how natural systems work.

Our Legacy of Mistreated Land

New Mexico history recalls, just over a century ago, when vast stands of grasses reached as high as a horse's chest. Near water, big bluestem and other tall prairie grasses stood 8 to 12 feet tall. Within these grassland communities, hundreds of plant, animal, and insect species (down to the last soil microbe) lived together in a happy, extended family. Now the animals are mostly gone, and the healthiest plant specimens are often tucked into highway or railroad right-of-ways, and in neglected cemeteries. Even against the backdrop of a 70,000 year trend of growing aridity, New Mexico's grasslands have been unquestionably heavily impacted by humans.

What happened? Ponderosa pines (relics from earlier, moister eras) were logged out, along with many piñons. Huge chains were dragged across some areas, ripping out junipers and piñons, to encourage grass production for livestock. Sheep and cattle selectively ate their way through their favorite plants, leaving behind only stunted grasses and unpalatables such as cholla and snakebroom. The trampled land eroded, and became less able to absorb what little water fell here. With large pieces of the community gone or damaged, the supporting cast of animals, insects, etc., packed up and moved on. What's left is broken land.

A Maze of Cooperative Connections

Mature ecosystems are characterized by a diversity of species which form an intricate web of cooperative relationships, evolved over eons. The relationships themselves are the glue holding the system together. The more diversity there is, the more connections there are, and therefore the more stability. Life on earth is so much richer than the linear, Darwinian concept of "survival of the fittest."

Consider these vignettes illustrating the cooperative "whole system" model:

• Early morning bird song stimulates tiny openings on leaf surfaces to open, exchange gases and absorb moisture, resulting in greater growth.

• Plants need each other; some are even dubbed "nurse plants." Infant piñons are almost always found within the arms of a "nurse" juniper tree on its shady, north side.

• One of the more astonishing examples of cooperation comes from Kenya where it was found that as gazelles were returned to grasslands previously overgrazed by cattle, plant growth increased dramatically. Why? A gazelle's saliva contains hormones which stimulate the growth of those particular plants preferred by the animal.

Big Successes with Small Means

So if you are looking to heal nearly lifeless land, must you bring in animals, birds, worms, fungi, all the plants, and the rest? No. The relationships will restore themselves with the slightest support. We're not talking vast sums of money, heavy machinery, and loads of water, either. The bare bones of (one way to accomplish) this process are 1) getting the water to stay in the soil, 2) covering the land with mulch, and 3) throwing in some manure (or other microorganisms) to catalyze soil processes. Selective use of seeds and/or seedlings can speed up the process.

Many such projects (from 1/8 to 100 acres) are sprouting up all over the southwest. How well do they actually work? Fred Werth, of Santa Fe, finds land restoration a personally meaningful calling. Werth jumped at the chance to work on 30 acres of sparse, stunted grasses with the usual New Mexico history—logging, grazing, erosion. He added a new twist, though. In search of a truly sustainable model using only rainfall, he allowed new tree and shrub seedlings only one gallon of water at planting time, but put them in protective, deep pockets in swales (level ditches which can hold water, *see* page 12). On a dry, hot, windy October day, weeks after the last rain, I saw Werth stick his hand down deep into the swale and come up with a handful of wet straw. As he wrings it out, he talks about how less than 20 months after the project began airplane pilots were asking questions about "that green area in Galisteo..." Grasses on the 30 acres responded beautifully to a sprinkling of manure and relatively light mulch of straw, and are noticeably larger and healthier than those just over the property line.

Werth feels that the huge rift between most ranchers and ecologists might be healed if ranchers could regard the land from a broader perspective. He sees selective, well-timed grazing as only part of the whole picture. The rest could include trees and shrubs grown for nursery stock; harvests of grama grass straw bales (twice as good for reclaiming grasslands); food...There's really no limit to the productivity of well-cared-for land, as long as we fit into the web that's there, rather than imposing our notions on it.

Sol y Sombra is a 20 acre private estate, less than five miles from the Plaza in Santa Fe, designed as a model environmental education site for drylands. Though by no means a small project, just two years after extensive wildlife plantings, bird species increased from 36 to 59.

Setting aside these larger projects, even the most limited efforts have the potential to be very powerful, precisely because they are small, easily accomplished, and because they capture the minds and hearts of all who witness them. In Werth's words, "Everyone's taken from this land, and no one's given back." But when our vision extends beyond what's of benefit to us, everyone can win.

RESOURCES

Fred Werth, land restoration specialist, 551 Cordova Rd., Suite 432, Santa Fe, NM 87501, consults with landowners and reforestation investors.

The Permaculture Institute, 455-0270, can give referrals of people qualified to help with land restoration. *See* page 55-56 for further information.

Coming to Grips:
ONE VIEW OF THE PATH FORWARD

(This article appeared as a companion piece to a review on The Dying of the Trees, *by Charles Little.)*

If Jim Cummings' review (or the prospect of reading Charles Little's book) depresses or frightens you, you're normal, and you're not alone. Reading them makes it clear that our collective fate is intertwined among the fungi surrounding tree roots—as well as directly linked with the waste products of an over-consumptive industrial society.

I believe the present challenge is for ordinary people to learn to see and think in new ways: in terms of whole systems, alive in *every* component, where earthworms are respected as much as humans. This could well be the most difficult, yet most inspiring work we've ever done.

But our society has nursed a favored myth that might read like this: "We humans are God's special creation, on an earth made specifically for our needs and desires. What's more, it's our destiny to conquer, master and shape nature (nature being like a wild beast to be tamed). Our ingenuity is boundless, as is our ability to solve any problem."

In our cleverness, we've learned to name, categorize, analyze, predict and prove, but these data contribute little to wisdom and a path which preserves our home. With a proliferation of specialists unable to see how parts interact and connect into whole systems, what do we do now?

I don't think the old tools and myths that got us into this mess are adequate to bail us out. How do we find new ethical principles on which to base an inspiring, juicy vision which, instead of seeing everything through the filter of what humans gain, reaches towards interconnection with *all* beings in the world?

We begin by asking the broadest, most difficult questions we can find: What's the best use of my life, time and energy, right now, to address our problems? How might I allow the southwest to shape me? What unseen forces are driving my habits, my life? Is there any such thing as a purely local problem?

Perhaps you and I can begin to take the pulse of the planet ourselves, with common sense as the primary tool. My approach is to join groups and classes with others, becoming a student of this place, its soils, flora, fauna, history, and ecosystems. I find it enriching and exhilarating to join in dialogue with others. My eyes have been opened to options I couldn't see before, to errors in my thinking, to the extent to which I'm still embedded in this society's way of looking at things. All this has led to a feeling of community support for making necessary changes, satisfying group action, a sense of great energy and creativity, and the birth of some new social forms. Direct contact with the earth affords practical lessons and the juice to keep it all going.

And thus, the new vision begins to be fleshed out.

Your approach may be different. Each person's contribution will be unique, and we need them all as we feel our way along this new path.

But how can we bear to deal with the devastating prognosis of our beloved planet? First off, look it squarely in the face, and feel the pain—pain which our eternally hopeful culture says must be avoided at all costs. (Don't do it alone.) We need more than anything to reject the idea that our problems are so big, so complicated, that we are powerless in the face of them. Indeed, just to name them is empowering. Once we admit what's *really* happening, the doors are opened, and out comes deep caring and courage, and the possibility of astounding shifts of consciousness.

It's instructive to look at how the body heals *its* wounds: islands of specialized tissue are formed which gradually grow to meet other islands, closing the wound. Could each bioregion on earth serve as an island of health in a healing world?

The cutting edge in medicine reveals the human body in constant communication with itself. I believe the earth, too, is conscious, engrossed in similar communication. Perhaps we could arrange a meeting.

I won't lie to you and say this work doesn't have its bittersweet aspects— always in the back of my mind is a prayer that it's not too late. Charles Little closes his powerful book by invoking the words of William Wordsworth, and says that the only antidote to despair is to stay firm in the belief that "nature never did betray the heart that loved her."

May we all fall deeply in love as soon as possible.

LIVING LIGHTLY ON THE EARTH:
How One Group Moved Beyond Talk to Action

A small group of imaginative, spirited people gather together in Santa Fe each month with a clearly defined commitment: To take concrete actions, large and small, to live more lightly on this earth (i.e., to use less and pollute less). They are using innovative tools to achieve their goals, including a cooperative loan fund that is already producing results.

This group (yes, I'm a member) formed in 1996, growing slowly and organically out of a series of much smaller meetings dating back to 1991. We called ourselves "Sustainable Presence" and set our upper limit at 30 members. (We've since stabilized at around 20, a much more manageable number.) Of course, "sustainable" has become one of those buzzwords that's beginning to lose its meaning. Simply put, it's living in a way so there's something worthwhile left for the grandchildren (as well as folks who will be here thousands of years from now).

We defined the vision of Sustainable Presence:

• To take personal responsibility to make changes in our private lives that benefit the environment and conserve resources, ultimately enriching the Santa Fe area.

• To form our own cooperative loan fund to facilitate major purchases that could make a real difference in an individual's energy and resource use.

• To create a presence in the community that might inspire others to launch their own experiments in sustainable living.

• Within our group, to share knowledge and resources, to learn new skills, and to nurture trust and effective communication.

• To have a hell of a good time doing all of the above.

How the Cooperative Loan Fund Works

Most but not all Sustainable Presence members are participanting. Each person joins the coop for a full share ($70) or a half share ($35). This amount is deposited each month into a group account. Whenever the balance grows to $3,000, we throw names into a hat of those who are ready to put the money to use. (A whole share award is $3,000, a half share $1,500.) Members are awarded a loan only once. Over roughly three-and-a-half years, every member will get back either $1,500 or $3,000—exactly what he or she put into the fund.

Here are some examples from our list of acceptable items on which to spend the loan money: Insulation for walls or roof to reduce winter energy use; rainwater storage systems (from 1,000-12,000 gallons); resource-saving appliances such as energy-efficient refrigerators, washing machines and compact fluorescent light bulbs; solar panels; composting and low flush toilets; modification of autos and trucks to accept propane fuel (less polluting than gasoline); and electric auto conversion kit for small cars (imagine using no gasoline!).

The cost of some of these items is substantial enough that the ordinary citizen would balk at spending the money, but the loan cooperative makes buying them a doable option.

Loan recipients become borrowers from the Sustainable Presence community. They make their purchase within three months, spend the entire loan on sustainables (including labor for installation) and give an accounting to the group of how the money was spent. The borrower simply continues to make payments each month, as before, with no interest. As one member put it, "I had a budget for everything else *but* purchases to make my home more efficient and sustainable. Now it's so easy and fun to save with the group."

Receiving an interest-free loan of $1,500 or $3,000 from one's friends is a real rush and leads to serious bonding. I was the first recipient of a loan, which I used for a series of tanks that store 1,300 gallons of rainwater runoff from my roof.

Since we meet at different homes each month, we can admire tanks full of rainwater, peer into energy-saving, state-of-the-art refrigerators that shear megabucks off the electric bill, and see what it's really like to live with compact fluorescent bulbs. As more members receive their loans, we hope to ride in an electric vehicle and make deposits into our friends' composting toilets.

This path is not without its difficulties. Sometimes we feel like alternative technology guinea pigs, humoring temperamental solar storage batteries, and the like. The risks are more than worth it ... making changes while supported by 20 people is empowering.

Growing Pains

The expansion of the group, on the other hand, brought considerable growing pains. A bunch of adults, four or five kids and a dog or two in a living room can lead to more chaos than communication. We wonder how to recover the sweet flavor of intimacy and thoughtful exploration of issues that was the hallmark of the original smaller groups, while expanding our focus to include outward action. Though discomforts with differing needs and styles of communication do arise, shared goals keep us committed to the challenge of learning to listen, work, play and communicate in community. However, this is literally, by choice, a leaderless group and that produces its own set of problems.

We All Benefit Together

An extremely satisfying activity of the group is improving the lands we inhabit. Most of us live in semi-rural settings. Once a season, we assemble at the home of whoever needs help and enhance the earth by planting native grass seed or tree seedlings, mulching, preparing soil for a vegetable garden, creating erosion control on slopes, etc. People learn valuable skills that can be applied to their own land or taught to others.

In between our potluck meetings, we support each other in many ways— providing dinners for a week to parents of a new baby, attending a member's art opening, pitching in to help someone move, sitting in the audience while a member speaks at a public hearing, and so on. Being there for each other breaks down the sense of isolation so pervasive in our individualistic society.

So what does all this add up to? Hopefully, a powerful antidote to frustration and despair in the face of enormous problems. Even if you're an urban renter, you could craft a similar plan for creating sustainability and mutual support in your community.

RESOURCES

Real Goods Trading Corporation, 555 Leslie St., Ukiah, CA 95482, (800) 762-7325. They publish the bible of sustainability buffs, the *SolarLiving Sourcebook*, $30.00. It contains generous amounts of information and articles not only on solar technology, but about toilets, vehicles, tools, household products—all you need to know to get your home scene together. You can also explore their interactive website, *www.realgoods.com.*

Inspiration for the loan fund was sparked by a member's attendance at **The Bioneers Conference,** where the focus is on practical strategies to restore our earth and communities. The Bioneers Conference is a project of the **Collective Heritage Institute.** which conducts educatonal programs and research in the areas of biodiversity, ecological farming practices and environmental restoration. For more information about their work, to receive their newsletter, or for membership, write to CHI, 901 W. San Mateo Rd., Suite L, Santa Fe, NM 87505, call (505) 986-0366, toll-free 1-877-BIONEER, or visit their website at *www.bioneers.org.*

SANTA FE GROWS A FIRST-CLASS BOTANICAL GARDEN

For 11 years, members of the Santa Fe Botanical Garden have been dying to get a certain kind of dirt under their fingernails. Though it looked in 1997 like they had secured a permanent site at Santa Fe Community College for the formal gardens, by early 1999, final plans ran into some serious snags. But no matter where the garden eventually lands, it won't be ordinary; its members are certain it will be a major destination on the botanical garden circuit.

Strong Links to the Community

First, the conventional part: the Santa Fe Botanical Garden will include elements often found at such institutions—collections of endangered plants, display gardens, classrooms, a library, an herbarium where dried, pressed plants are catalogued, etc. And its mission is similar to that of many botanical gardens—"to conserve, cultivate, study and display plant species within all ecosystems and ethnic cultures of our bioregion, and to provide opportunities for botanical education."

But it's *how* the Garden plans to accomplish its mission that sets it apart from most other botanical gardens. Here are some of the innovative features:

• Test plots to demonstrate organic and sustainable agriculture methods for local farmers

• "Therapy gardens" where troubled youth and adults create beautiful gardens while "getting grounded" in the dirt

• A network of community gardens, orchards and "pocket parks." The Garden will provide technical support; the people living nearby will create and maintain the gardens.

Thus, the Botanical Garden won't be some abstract place for "plant people." It will be part of people's everyday lives. Michael Clark, one of the Garden's founders and owner of Jackalope Nursery, foresees "sites all over the city, and a presence at the railyards." As soon as the city opened up the design process on the railyards' historic 57-acre central location, members of the Botanical Garden board were quick to offer their vision of a 10-acre arboretum and plenty of green on the other 47 acres.

There's a Muskrat in the Classroom!

Probably the most unconventional aspect of this Garden is the concept of "natural history sites." These areas will demonstrate the ecosystems of our region, such as high desert, riparian (river or pond), forest, etc. But rather than being at the college, these are outlying sites with interpretive trails. This arrangement gives a better understanding of the whole systems in which plants are found, and provides living classrooms with vivid learning experiences.

In 1993, the Garden acquired its first site, the Leonora Curtin Natural History Area—35 exquisitely beautiful acres adjacent to the Spanish colonial museum, El Rancho de las Golondrinas, south of Santa Fe. It is one of the few remaining examples in New Mexico of the *cienega* (marsh land) ecosystem. Though relatively intact, there has been loss of some plant species, and a lowering of the water table, making reseeding of cottonwoods improbable.

For four years, this area has served as an outdoor laboratory for elementary through college level classes, and provides opportunities for species inventories, water monitoring studies, and research on how animals and insects interrelate with plant communities. Children learn unforgettable lessons among egrets, painted turtles, muskrats and towering cottonwoods. College students in wetlands or bioremediation courses conduct trials of land restoration techniques and get graphic feedback.

Healing damaged areas is an interest of many Garden members. At this site, Russian Olive, an aggressive, non-native species is being thinned out, while 75 willows and cottonwoods have been planted. As hillside erosion is controlled, grasses reseeded, and the eight seeps and springs are shaded, the water table in this *cienega* may come up to previous levels. Stuff like this really turns naturalists on.

Nature is the Best Teacher

Bill Isaacs, an early supporter of the Garden, generated an unending stream of fresh visions. Naturalist, botanist, educator, wallking field guide for birds, plants, mushrooms, geology and more, Isaacs' death in early 1997 saddened Garden members. I spoke with him several months before his death.

Isaacs lived near the Galisteo River for years. As grazing was reduced, he noted the beginning of the river's recovery. "I was walking down the river and heard a Northern Chat [a bird]. The Chat is an indicator species found in pristine or recovering watersheds. It indicated how quickly the environment restores itself when given the opportunity."

This experience inspired him to develop a wetlands natural history area for the Botanical Garden. (He later became Curator of the Leonora Curtin site.) "There's constructed wetlands everywhere, everybody's experts in measuring this and doing that. But I'm interested in how nature does it, because

I don't think we're that smart. Watching a system naturally stitch itself back together again tells me an awful lot more about what we need to do."

Formidable Grass Roots

Even though they're still working on manifesting a home base, Garden members are not idle: they teach classes, lead field trips, and refine and nurture their vision. Now over 700 members strong, the Garden has connections with a huge network of like-minded organizations and people, all brimming with ideas and energy.

It is the Santa Fe Botanical Garden's fervent wish to play an integral part in the planning and future viability of the entire Santa Fe region. If any group could do it, this one could, through its cooperative projects with diverse environmental groups, broad community appeal, and juicy dreams.

RESOURCES

The Santa Fe Botanical Garden, a non-profit, private organization, relies on membership fees and donations. To join or to receive a copy of the newsletter, call 428-1684, or write P.O. Box 23343, Santa Fe, NM 87502-3343.

The Garden offers many activities, including garden tours, "walks and talks," lectures, classes and more.

✿ ✿ ✿

UPDATE, summer 2001: The Santa Fe Botanical Garden finally acquired land at Aldea de Santa Fe!

INDEX